The Supervisor

THE LIBRARY OF EDUCATION

A Project of The Center for Applied Research in Education, Inc.

G. R. Gottschalk, Director

Categories of Coverage

I	II	III
Curriculum and Teaching	Administration, Organization, and Finance	Psychology

IV	V	VI
History, Philosophy, and Social Foundations	Professional Skills	Educational Institutions

The Supervisor

ROBERT C. McKEAN

Professor of Education
University of Colorado

H. H. MILLS, *1898 –* Hubert Howard

Professor of Education
University of Colorado

The Center for Applied Research in Education, Inc.
Washington, D.C.

Foreword

In this volume on the supervisor are embodied many factors of importance to educators and laymen who seek quality education in their schools. These schools are caught up in a maelstrom of change. There are rapid changes in teaching personnel; student bodies are changing both in number and in nature; knowledge is changing in content and in direction; beliefs as to how to improve learning are changing; communities have changed their demands upon the schools. As the size of school units increases, individual teachers can get lost in this maze of change.

Professors McKean and Mills effectively combine their experiences and educational insights. They show how supervision has emerged from the early emphasis upon weeding out the deficient to the current challenge which seeks to help teachers become more efficient. As they examine the responsibilities and the qualifications of supervisory personnel, they formulate both principles and practices which are important in the resolution of today's critical problems in educational supervision. Values inherent in the group process, conditions necessary for effective group work, and some cautions are ably presented. Careful attention is also given to working with individual teachers.

The modern supervisor is presented as a democratic leader, as a coordinator, as a resource person, and as one in a strategic position to pull together the threads of evaluation. Above all, he is a social engineer seeking to enhance the personal strengths and the interpersonal relationships of the educational staff. Titles such as "helping teacher," "resource teacher," "consultant," and "coordinator" reflect some of the changes in his role.

In the concluding chapter on "Appraisal of the Supervisor's Work" the authors emphasize those facets of appraisal which they deem most significant in helping the reader develop new insights. How do we measure pupil learning? How does the teacher decide upon methods and materials? How is the necessary teacher morale assessed? How do teachers and supervisors evaluate themselves? The approaches to these questions as well as the rationale for the entire discussion make this an exciting book.

A volume such as *The Supervisor* should command careful study by interested educators. They should find that this compact volume bears out the McKean-Mills' contention that teachers working with the type of supervisor which they envision "should develop more confidence in themselves, feel more adequate to handle their own problems, and experience the fuller realization of their capabilities." This is a long step toward quality education.

ALBERT I. OLIVER

Chairman, Secondary School Division
Graduate School of Education
University of Pennsylvania

The Supervisor

Robert C. McKean
H. H. Mills

The Supervisor is a keystone volume in the Library of Education among those devoted to administrative and supervisory personnel and services in school systems. With this and other books in the series on educational administration and supervision, including the volumes on *In-Service Education for Teachers* and *The College President,* the Library gives extensive coverage of the several administrative and supervisory positions and functions.

This volume emphasizes the nature of modern supervision; the responsibilities of supervisory personnel in school systems and in the individual school; the desirable qualifications of supervisors; group procedures in supervision; desirable supervisory practices; and ways and means of appraising the supervisor's work.

The authors have written an up-to-date, authoritative, and forward-looking volume which will be helpful in planning for improvement of educational programs and processes.

WALTER A. ANDERSON
Content Editor

Contents

CHAPTER VIII

Appraisal of the Supervisor's Work   101

CHAPTER I

The Nature of the Supervisory Process

The supervisor has become an important agent in the continuing efforts to sustain excellence in teaching and learning in the public schools of today. Supervision, however, is not a single, unitary function, nor is it accomplished solely by a person or persons who conveniently bear the title "supervisor." Supervision, instead, is multiple, complex, and often intangible. It is the product and responsibility of many educational personnel.

The Evolving Concept of the Role of Supervision

A study of the historical changes in American education reveals a dramatic shift in the conception and practice of supervision. The overall aim of supervision, however, has remained remarkably consistent from the first crude beginnings during the colonial days to some of the most sophisticated and complicated programs of today. Through the years efforts have been directed toward the general aim of ensuring and improving the quality of instruction.

As improved educational theory and practices have evolved, so have very different approaches to supervision developed. New and vital bodies of knowledge regarding the nature of the growth and development of children, the essential conditions of learning and teaching, and ways of working in groups emerged and received consideration. Factors which contributed to this evolution were the changing nature and conditions of American society, shifting expectations of the proper role of public elementary and secondary education in our culture, and increasingly complex organizational and personnel patterns found in the schools.

Early concept—autocratic, inspection. Public concern for the nature and quality of instruction in the schools manifested itself early in the history of education in the United States. Initial attempts at supervision were marked by an emphasis on autocratic inspection. Laymen set standards and through examinations and visitation sought to weed out teachers who were judged to be deficient.

A rudimentary form of supervision made its appearance shortly after the establishment of schools in the New England colonies. Since the religious motive was predominant in these schools, the supervisory activities were directed not only at "protecting" the pupils from the incompetence of poorly trained teachers, but also at shielding them from religious unorthodoxy. Efforts were made to achieve the latter purpose through an arrangement by which local members of the clergy interviewed and examined applicants for teaching positions to ascertain the soundness of their religious beliefs and practices. These clergymen also visited the schools to assess the instruction in terms of the prevailing religious faith of the community.

The first provision for supervision by official school representatives was authorized in 1654 by a statute of the General Court of Massachusetts Bay Colony. Under the law the selectmen of the towns were given the responsibility for appointing teachers of "sound faith and morals" to work in the schools under their jurisdiction. The selectmen were also charged with the responsibility of retaining these teachers in their positions only as long as they conducted their schools in keeping with the accepted religious precepts. In the discharge of their duties it was necessary for these committees to visit each of the schools to scrutinize the teacher's conduct, observe the pupils' behavior, question the pupils closely, and examine their written work.

As the schools became larger, thus necessitating the employment of two or more teachers, one of the teachers was designated as head or principal teacher and assumed some of the responsibilities formerly held exclusively by the selectmen. This plan represented the beginning of a limited amount of managerial control by a person within the school itself. These principal teachers, however, were not relieved of their own full schedule of teaching duties.

Thus the pattern of supervision as inspection to ascertain the deficiencies of teachers was established, and the early supervisor's role was based upon the premise that there were known and fixed methods of teaching which could be identified and judged by a brief observation of the teacher's work. If any consideration were given to the improvement of the teacher's work, it was based upon the assumption that an inspection might prompt the teacher to do better work. This early concept of supervision appears very narrow and inadequate in the light of our present knowledge of human growth and development. These early endeavors, however, should be evaluated in terms of the accepted philosophy of education and the limited knowledge of the learning process that existed in the seventeenth century.

Another phase in the development of supervisory programs began with the creation of the position of superintendent of schools. The first state superintendent of schools in the United States was appointed in New York under the provisions of a law of 1812 which authorized the establishment of a state department of education. The first city school superintendents were appointed in 1837 in Buffalo, New York, and Louisville, Kentucky. By 1870 there were superintendents in the 29 largest cities in the United States. For many years these superintendents devoted their time chiefly to administrative and clerical duties. As these duties increased with the growth of the school population, the superintendents delegated some supervisory duties to assistants. Thus a division of administrative and supervisory functions began.

Perhaps the chief supervisory contribution of the school superintendents in the first years after their positions were established was in the leadership many of them exercised in organizing programs for the upgrading of the education of teachers in service. These programs took the form of county institutes. The first of these institutes was held in Connecticut in 1839. The institutes were designed primarily to provide instruction for the teachers in the common school subjects they had been assigned to teach. The teachers were required by law in most states to attend the institutes, usually for a period of a week each year. This endeavor to improve instruction, however, did not replace the inspectional side of supervision in the local schools. The emphasis on teaching subject matter shifted somewhat to include methods of teaching in the last two decades before the institutes were discontinued in the 1920's.

With the addition of new subjects such as music and home economics to the school curriculum in the period from 1875 to 1900, it soon became evident that few teachers were qualified to teach these subjects. Consequently, special subject supervisors were appointed in many school systems to assist teachers of these subjects.

Many of these supervisors had the responsibility for working with teachers in several schools in a particular area within a school system. They were assigned to the central office and traveled from class to class, often actually teaching the subjects as well as helping the regular teachers gain some minimal competency.

When the need for rural school supervision emerged, the task was assigned to general supervisors. These elementary school experts were often a part of the office of the county superintendent of schools and worked under his direction. Small rural schools without sufficient resources to provide supervisory help for themselves were served from a nearby, but larger, organizational unit. The general supervisor in this case had little authority to lay down directives and enforce their observance. Thus the supervisory and administrative functions became even more separated.

After the first public high school was established in 1821, legal moves paved the way for enhanced tax support for a system of public education from elementary school through college. Subsequent pressures and conditions in American society caused great increases in school enrollment. As a result of this growth in the size of the school and of the teaching staff, the building principal was released from teaching duties and took on more complex administrative responsibilities. Soon experienced teachers were appointed by the principal to supervise more inexperienced teachers and to carry out a minimum of administrative tasks along with their regular teaching assignments. Thus the position of department head was created and was expected to contribute to the improvement of instruction.

Along with the increase in size of schools and school districts came the appointment of a variety of special and general supervisors. Persons for these supervisory positions were chosen because of their competence in teaching and their ability to inspect and rate teachers.

The transition from early efforts at supervision to present day practices and theory included several significant characteristics:

1. Supervision by religious and civil lay bodies was gradually replaced by supervision by professional personnel.
2. A growing concern developed over the difficulty in separating administrative functions from supervisory functions.
3. Two approaches to supervision appeared: general supervision and special supervision.

4. Supervisory activity was initiated and carried out at several levels —for example, within the school building unit, throughout the school district, and at the county and state levels.

Modern concept—scientific, democratic, creative. During the twentieth century the concept of supervision has been shaped by successive emphases on the application of the method and contributions of science in education, a preoccupation with the ideals of democracy, and the recognition that the elements of improved teaching lie within the teacher himself. Although the traditional inspectional and autocratic aspects of supervision have not disappeared, the modern supervisor embodies much of the newer viewpoint.

As the scientific movement in education gained impetus and favor, the influence was felt in supervisory practices. Teacher qualifications were specified; scientific measurements were utilized; data were secured and statistically analyzed; scientific methods of teaching were sought and encouraged; and research and experimentation were instituted. This approach gave supervision a more objective, experimental flavor. Judgments regarding the improvement of learning and teaching depended less upon sheer opinion and more upon the relevant data which could be secured.

During the 1930's an awakening interest in the possibilities of cooperation and a reaction against the severely autocratic nature of traditional supervision led to a more democratic approach. The supervisor attempted to operate as a leader rather than as a director. Teacher cooperation and participation were sought in determining, exploring, and solving problems. This movement brought increased respect for the teacher as an individual and emphasized teacher perception and involvement as essential factors in the work of supervision.

Subsequent attention was given to the task of finding ways to release the potential residing within the individual teacher. This effort was based on the assumption that the most significant improvements to instruction come as the teacher fulfills his own promise and finds within himself the means to better teaching. The supervisor aimed to stimulate, encourage, and guide this creativity.

The modern concept of supervision includes elements of all these points of view. Some idea of the resulting combination is revealed in a representative statement of guidelines for modern supervision.[1]

1. Instructional supervision is a dynamic, growing process that is occupying an increasingly important role in the schools.
2. The purpose of supervision is to offer leadership in the improvement of educational experiences for children and youth.
3. Leadership is centered in a group, not in an individual.
4. The type and quality of supervision are affected by the situation, the organization, in which the supervision exists.
5. The climate of human relationships within the group and the degree to which members are committed to group goals influence the degree of change in practice.
6. The way in which individuals perceive the problems and the tasks in the situation affects their behavior.
7. The actual role of supervision—and of instructional leaders—is a composite of all the expectations held for the role by the people associated with it.
8. A primary goal of supervisory leaders is to foster leadership in others.

Thus it is clear that the supervisor of today works toward the improvement of learning and teaching as did the supervisor of yesterday. He seeks, however, to provide the sort of educational leadership which will impel teachers to strive for improvement, and he fosters experimentation and cooperative effort to this end. He aims for the fulfillment of the teachers' latent potentialities so that they may make a fuller contribution to this vital overall goal. The supervisor is concerned with the entire learning-teaching situation and he works with and through other educational personnel.

Current Need

Supervision has grown in importance over the years because of real and pressing educational needs. Currently, a number of existing conditions places supervision in an even more strategic position in our schools.

Teachers today are faced with an ever broadening complexity of the educational task. In the modern elementary and secondary school, learning and teaching are more broadly conceived than ever

---

[1] R. M. Burnham and Martha L. King, *Supervision in Action* (Washington, D.C.: Association for Supervision and Curriculum Development, National Education Association, 1961), p. 32.

before. Teachers not only impart knowledge, but they are also expected to inculcate attitudes, develop essential skills, strengthen loyalties, promote allegiance to our way of life, and reinforce moral codes. Moreover, they attempt this multiple teaching objective with the understanding that other educative agencies in American society share the task of providing the total education of youth. The home, the church, mass media of communication, youth groups, and other educative forces have profound influences upon the broad range of educational objectives. Some of these forces complement the work of the school while others operate in competition with the teacher.

The impressive growth in school enrollment has brought large numbers of students with which the school must deal. As the expectation of education through high school grew in acceptance, great heterogeneity in pupils resulted at all levels. Wide ranges of academic aptitude, socio-economic background, interests, abilities, special talents, and educational expectations are prevalent. Thus teachers must meet unprecedented instructional demands.

The expanding horizons in knowledge and the accumulation of data and information challenge the teacher to attain and uphold expertness. The high school physics instructor, for example, can hardly teach competently year after year without a continuing program of reading and study to keep up to date in his subject.

In education itself new developments in teaching procedures, in staff organization and use, and in learning materials and resources constantly require study and appraisal. Teachers need to keep informed of trends and new directions in this specialized body of professional knowledge. They also need to participate in the research and experimentation which result in contributions to this knowledge and which may refine and improve their personal teaching efforts. Teaching machines, programmed textbooks, television teaching, language laboratories, and team teaching are only a few of the more dramatic developments which may affect the nature and role of the teacher.

The increasing size of schools and teaching staffs, the greater mobility of the instructional force, and the large number of beginning teachers indicate the need for more supervisory effort. Teachers new to the system require careful orientation. Beginning teachers particularly need assistance in developing skill, and all personnel appreciate the opportunity to establish satisfying and productive relationships in the complicated educational systems of today. Great need is felt for integration and coordination of the activities and resources of the various professional personnel in order to carry out the purposes of the school.

Today as never before the services of supervisors are necessary to continued educational progress. The need is apparent; the overall aim is clear; and fruitful ways of working are being developed.

Functions of Supervisory Services

The modern supervisor finds it necessary to work with many persons at different levels. The work of supervision, however, may be roughly divided into four general functions: leadership, coordination, resource and service, and evaluation.

Leadership. The supervisor should encourage the emergence and acceptance of leadership in others as well as exert supervisory leadership himself.

According to Swearingen [2] there are at least five facets of supervisory leadership in a democracy: (1) exerting initiative, (2) aiding in goal setting, (3) stimulating and releasing talents, (4) supporting teachers while change is under way, and (5) following through on group commitments. The supervisor may identify problems, perform preliminary surveys, assess teacher or parental concern, collate evidence, and bring groups together as an aspect of his leadership role. He may help clarify teacher purposes and aims and work for agreement in philosophy. He may seek to extend the vision of teachers, to remove some of the blocks which impede progress, and to encourage satisfying contributions by individuals. The supervisor may attempt to establish a climate which is favorable to change and which is supportive to those involved. He may need to carry out such matters as writing summaries, completing reports, distributing materials and arranging subsequent meetings. All this and more falls within the function of leadership.

The supervisor, at the same time he is seeking through personal effort and example to encourage teachers to strive for improved productivity, should remain alert to emerging initiative and leadership in others. He should be careful not to ignore or smother po-

---

[2] Mildred E. Swearingen, *Supervision of Instruction: Foundations and Dimensions* (Boston: Allyn and Bacon, Inc., 1962), p. 54.

tential leadership. School organizations marked by sustained and vital progress depend upon the contributions of emergent leadership among their members.

Coordination. Within the various levels of school organization there are many resources and energies which need to be organized and brought to bear upon important problems. Educational supervision may make important contributions within the school district, within the elementary or secondary school building, and among individual teachers. At times the supervisor may work in the community itself.

Coordination involves such important tasks as locating and organizing educational resources and making them available to persons who need and want them. The supervisor successfully engages the staff in cooperative endeavor and encourages it to seek even more satisfying group work. He also facilitates the essential contributions of parents and students at appropriate points. An overall perspective and a clear grasp of the educational aims are essential to the function of coordination.

Resource and service. The supervisor himself is a resource. His experience, training, and skills are placed at the disposal of the school. His own acquaintance with the results of current experimentation, his professional expertness, and his skills in human relations contribute to efficiency and success in solving problems. The supervisor often assists the top administrator and the school board in making important policies and judgments. He may also be called upon to help interpret the aims, procedures, and results of the school program to the public.

Evaluation. The function of evaluation is basic to supervision. Improvement and progress have their beginnings in the appraisal of present conditions. Moreover, the emphasis on evaluation needs to be continuous and far reaching.

Supervisors work with others to assess the appropriateness and worth of educational aims. This involves the definition of purposes, the establishment of pertinent criteria, and the application of these criteria to the stated goals of the school. Supervisory activity is directed toward the evaluation of learnings and the teaching procedures which go to produce them. The central function of the school itself is realized in the learning which takes place under the direction and guidance of the teacher in the classroom. Much assistance is needed to help teachers and students appraise the quality and productiveness of the learning-teaching process. In addition the educational personnel of the school require help in evaluating their group activities. The supervisor himself must constantly assess the outcomes of his efforts.

Authority in supervision. The role of the supervisor has many facets and demands, yet in order to carry out successfully his essential functions he must have some degree of authority. This authority may come to him in several different ways:

1. He may be delegated authority by the top administrator and the school board. This is legal authority to act in certain areas and in certain ways because of his position in the organization of the school.

2. The supervisor may earn a substantial degree of authority because of his competence. School personnel who work with him give him this authority because they recognize his expertness in the special knowledge and skills needed to accomplish improvement in the program of the school.

3. Finally the supervisor may be offered authority by specific groups within which he works. A group which has direction and purpose may assign various responsibilities to different members. In a situation marked by minimal status differences the supervisor may receive authority from the group itself to act in ways which seem likely to enhance the effective solution of problems and the accomplishment of group purposes. This authority is dynamic (having to do with direction and purpose) and temporary (developing out of and having pertinence to a specific situation).

As supervisors carry out their functions, they may at times rely on each of these sources of authority. Modern supervision, however, has come to emphasize the latter two sources of authority in its approach.

Principles of Modern Supervision

A number of important principles are inherent in today's concept of the supervisory process. Such principles provide a guide to action as well as an approach to the evaluation of procedures.

1. Supervision is directed toward the improvement of learning and teaching. This has remained the overall objective, and it provides the ultimate criterion in appraisal of successful supervision.

2. The total program of supervision is directed to accepted purposes.

Effective supervision seeks to help teachers recognize and accept general aims and then works consciously toward these purposes. For example, teachers may come to accept the proper role of supervision as a specialized service which attempts (a) to help them see beyond their present performance and seek improvement, (b) to identify and coordinate efforts and resources for more efficiency and greater impact on important educational problems, (c) to increase the amount and quality of learning by students, and (d) to promote continuous appraisal of performance of all who are engaged in the educational process.

3. Supervision seeks the cooperative participation of all concerned. Intelligent and effective supervision is genuine cooperative endeavor, not skillful manipulation of others. This principle results from the strong belief that school personnel affected by certain decisions should have a part in making these decisions.

4. Modern supervision strives to utilize the talents and strengths of all. The emerging concept of democratic leadership recognizes the necessity of releasing and using the potential which resides within various members of the group. The most effective group problem-solving results from the joint efforts of individuals, each making contributions in line with his own special abilities and skills.

5. The existing situation provides the setting for supervision. The nature and characteristics of the staff, the student group, the community, and the past and present school program are the basic elements with which the supervisor must deal. Thus he must know well the present situation and its antecedents before proceeding to make improvements.

6. Supervision offers assistance to all. The astute supervisor knows that the most likely places to begin are with those teachers who recognize needs and who are willing to work for improvement. He knows that often the teachers who seem to be doing the best job are those with greatest potential for sustained progress. He works with all, not merely the inexperienced or ineffective.

7. Supervision is flexible. The supervisor tends to be eclectic in approach. A concern about the means as well as the end requires a flexible, adaptive approach rather than adherence to a single "approved" procedure.

8. Supervision seeks evidence regarding the results and value of change. The supervisor uses his skills in evaluation to this end. Judgments should be based upon the weight of evidence and logic rather than upon hunch or sheer opinion.

9. Supervision strives to enhance the satisfaction in their work of the educational staff. The procedures of supervision should result in improved staff morale and job satisfaction. As a consequence of the work of the supervisor, teachers should develop more confidence in themselves, feel more adequate to handle their own problems, and experience the fuller realization of their capabilities.

Organization of Supervisory Services

The total supervisory effort is borne by many different persons operating at various organizational levels. Contributions to the improvement of instruction and learning may be made at the state level, the county level, the school system level, and the individual school level.

Most state departments of education are strongly committed to a program of supervision. Generally they are charged with the implementation of legislative acts and rulings of the state board of education. Thus they retain some responsibility for inspecting the schools through personal visits or through required reports. State accreditation of schools may involve cooperative study and visitation. Supervisory assistance, however, is increasingly being made available, especially to schools with limited resources. Central office supervisors coordinate state-wide efforts, identify resources and publicize them, inform school people regarding research, experimentation and promising practices emerging within the state, and offer direct assistance to schools, usually of a consultative nature. Many state departments of education have gained great potential power to affect school practices through their administration and distribution of state monies.

Strong county organizations have developed in a few states where the county superintendent of schools has been provided with financial resources and enabling legislation, thus permitting him to build a large staff of general and special supervisors and consultants. California, Florida, and Ohio are examples of states in which county offices are providing substantial supervisory assistance.

In local school systems the nature and extent of supervision is determined by the size of the administrative unit, the stability and quality of the educational staff, and the division of administrative and supervisory responsibilities. A small union high school district employing 25 teachers would probably have no supervision other than what the superintendent-principal and the part-time assistant principal could supply, while a large urban school system containing many elementary, junior high, and senior high schools might utilize a complex organization involving not only the local school personnel but also an assistant superintendent in charge of instruction, a director of curriculum, general elementary supervisors, and special supervisors of various subject areas. Occasionally, several small school districts may join forces to secure more supervisory assistance.

At the individual school level size is again an important factor. In any case the principal is directly responsible for the instruction in his school. In the elementary school he often is expected to act as general supervisor for the teachers. In the larger high school he may have the services of a coordinator of instruction and of various department heads. In addition, consultants from outside the school organization may be brought in to assist with supervision. Persons from colleges and universities and from commercial test and instructional materials companies are sometimes employed to work with teachers and planning groups on specific problems. Careful screening, special planning, and preparation are often necessary if these individuals are to make the maximum contribution as consultants.

Generally, the most productive supervision at all levels seems to result from consulting, coordinating, and helping approaches. For this reason full-time supervisory persons increasingly have become known as helping teacher, resource teacher, consultant, and coordinator. Present trends in staff organization and utilization indicate full-time supervisors are being given less administrative and directive responsibilities, such as rating teachers for tenure or prescribing instructional practices.

The organization of supervisory services naturally takes on different patterns according to the situation, the special strengths and weaknesses of the persons involved, and the philosophy of supervision which prevails. Thus it is understandable that great variability in organizational patterns exists. Even though some need is felt for more consistent and precise descriptions of supervisory positions, it seems inevitable that widely differing practices will continue to prevail.

CHAPTER II

Responsibilities of Supervisory Personnel
in a Local School System

The basic assumption underlying all supervision and administration activity in public education is that the schools exist for the
benefit of the student and the society in which he lives. The learning-
teaching situation is primary; all else is secondary and supportive
to this elemental process. Students are compelled to attend the public schools in order to learn, and teachers are employed to guide
and assist this learning. Without teachers and students there would
be no need for administrators and supervisors. Indeed, there would
be no need for schools. This assumption provides the vital perspective necessary for intelligently conceived supervision in the local
school system.

As school systems grow in size and complexity, the face-to-face
relationships between central office personnel and classroom teachers become less frequent. The top administrator and his staff are
likely to become more remote and inaccessible. The superintendent
who once directly supervised a small number of teachers in his
district may now head a large staff, many of whom have varying
responsibilities for supervision.

The Superintendent

The superintendent of schools is directly involved in supervision.
He is the executive officer of the school board and (subject to the
board's approval) the administrative head of the school system. It
is his task to conceive and construct a framework within which all
phases of school activity may operate successfully. Although his
concern with the instructional program itself is only one of many
responsibilities, it must be central, for he knows that ultimately the
only justification for himself and his staff is their contribution to
the basic work of the school—the learning-teaching process. Typi-

cally, he accepts the following kinds of supervisory responsibilities in the school system.

The superintendent builds a supervisory organization. In the United States the size and characteristics of school districts are tremendously varied. The superintendent of schools seeks an organization for supervisory services which (1) will clearly delineate assignment of responsibilities and duties, (2) will provide for communication and cooperation among the various persons involved, and (3) will be as simple and flexible as possible. Because of differences in school systems, the organizations chosen for supervision naturally display great differences in themselves.

In small systems which, however, are large enough to justify a full-time superintendent, the head administrator tends to work with the principals of the several schools in his district. He may engage in some face-to-face supervision of teachers. However, he must also carry the bulk of the load of administration in the system. Problems of communication among personnel are minimized because of close contact, yet the press of administrative duties reduces the time and attention which the superintendent can give to supervision. The organizational structure is simple and direct as contrasted to the sizable urban school system.

Large systems present many problems because of the complexity of relationships and sheer numbers of persons involved in supervision. Common organizational patterns may include the following characteristics: (1) dualism—where teachers are responsible to the principal of their school as well as to the supervisor in the central office; (2) line and staff—where the line of authority is distinct, from the superintendent down through assistant superintendent to principal to the teacher, while a number of staff persons offer highly specialized services; (3) coordinative—where the responsibility for the improvement of instruction is centered in an assistant superintendent of instruction (or in one holding a similar position) who coordinates the efforts of the principals and supervisors under his direction; and (4) democratic—where councils or committees of teachers and other educational personnel are brought into the exploration and solution of instructional problems.

Several trends seem evident in the current efforts of superintendents to secure improvement in existing supervisory organizations:

1. The desirable organizational change is looked upon as evolutionary in nature and is built upon the present organization.

2. Full-time supervisory personnel are increasingly seen as staff persons who work most productively without substantial line authority.

3. The teacher himself must be affected before change takes place in his classroom, thus the organization should facilitate teacher participation in sharing with administrative and supervisory personnel the task of upgrading learning and teaching.

4. The building as a vital unit in change is being re-emphasized by making the principal and his staff directly accountable to the superintendent or to the assistant superintendent in charge of instruction for program improvement, and by emphasizing the use of central office supervisors as consultants to building personnel in joint efforts to improve instruction.

The superintendent selects and retains personnel. One of the superintendent's important responsibilities, which has many supervisory implications, is the selection and retention of well-qualified personnel. He shares this responsibility with the principal of the individual school. In small districts the superintendent is likely to be directly involved in teacher recruitment and employment. In this case it is his responsibility to secure teachers who are not only the best he can obtain but also those who show promise of fitting into the supervisory philosophy of the school. For example, if the supervision is democratic in orientation and process, he will search for teachers who are likely to work well on committees and groups and who will gain satisfaction from this participation. The superintendent must also find ways to retain promising and productive teachers through rewards both financial and otherwise.

Central office personnel are always a direct responsibility of the superintendent. He must know his own organization and present personnel as well as the aims and objectives of the supervisory program, and he must secure the right persons to fit into this situation.

The superintendent sets the supervisory climate. The superintendent constructs the organizational framework for supervision. He also sets the spirit and atmosphere of the supervisory procedures. The whole supervisory function takes on the character of the superintendent's attitude. An autocratic, dictatorial superintendent is likely to produce a similar approach to supervision. A democratic superintendent is likely to create supervisory services which prize cooperation, originality, and self-initiative. In the right climate school personnel are often able and willing to rise above defects in the organization and make superior progress toward instructional improvement.

The superintendent motivates supervision. The top administrator may motivate supervisory effort by displaying interest and understanding of current efforts to improve instruction. His own knowledge of the program of the school and its effectiveness, his expressed concern regarding apparent weaknesses, and his encouragement to certain supervisory activity will impel supervisors to action. He is likely to influence supervision through giving rewards, such as promotions and praise, to productive personnel. Many superintendents consider it essential that they maintain a consistent and high degree of interest in the programs of instructional improvement in their school systems.

The superintendent evaluates supervision. The evaluation of the effectiveness and progress of the system's supervisory services is an important responsibility. The superintendent must make provisions for evaluating supervisory personnel. In some cases he will evaluate directly the work of his staff. In other cases he will assign this task to an assistant. In any event he will be concerned with an appraisal of efforts to improve teaching in the system. Often he is able to make a special contribution to the evaluative process because of his perspective and broad understanding of the system-wide program and the community within which it exists.

The Assistant Superintendent in Charge of Instruction

In larger school systems it is common to find the position of assistant superintendent in charge of instruction. The person who bears this title ranks next to the superintendent in the responsibility for the supervisory program of the school.

Generally the assistant superintendent in charge of instruction assumes the direct responsibility and leadership for (1) working toward a system-wide agreement regarding purposes of education, (2) coordinating the efforts of all persons dealing with the instructional program, (3) heading the continuous curriculum development and revision program in the system, (4) seeking ways to improve articulation among the educational segments, (5) encouraging emergent leadership among district personnel, and (6) striving to improve the organization and working relationships of personnel involved in the supervision of instruction.

The assistant superintendent in charge of instruction must, of course, establish and maintain close communication with the superintendent of schools. One of his tasks is to make sure that his decisions and ways of working are consistent with the policies of the superintendent and school board. He must see to it that the broad division of services in his charge moves forward along the lines established by the superintendent. He needs to apprise the top administrator about studies under way, programs for improvement instituted, and progress being achieved. In addition, as an assistant superintendent, he should attempt to establish good working relationships with other assistant superintendents in charge of other divisions of school system operation.

He may be directly in charge of the staff of supervisors who are assigned to the superintendent's office. In this event he supervises and coordinates their activities. Often the assistant superintendent in charge of instruction will conduct regular meetings of the principals to consider instructional problems. This places him in a strategic position to facilitate cooperative relationships between building principals and supervisors.

The Director of
Curriculum and Instruction

In large city school systems with many schools to serve, the staff of the superintendent of schools often includes persons who are known as the director of elementary education, director of secondary education, or director of curriculum and instruction. This position is commonly created to fulfill the need for more intensive direction of areas of responsibility under the general control of the assistant superintendent in charge of instruction. The director is responsible to the assistant superintendent. He is often approximately equal in rank to the building principals and, therefore, works with them on a cooperative basis rather than in a directive role.

The director of curriculum and instruction normally is in charge of the central office staff of supervisors and consultants. As such he has the responsibility for overseeing their work. He holds regular staff meetings to discuss their problems and concerns. He plans the orientation of new supervisors and provides for the in-service growth of all his staff. The director must organize the supervisory services under his control and constantly evaluate their effectiveness. He works to define duties and ways of working with teachers and principals. He attempts to promote the concept of central office supervision as a consultative, cooperative service. He usually holds the concept that his staff should offer specialized assistance which is so valuable and necessary that the principals will feel a real need to request it at appropriate points. In addition, the director of curriculum and instruction channels information regarding the supervisory activities, progress, and achievements through the assistant superintendent to the superintendent. When possible he seeks face-to-face contacts with principals and teachers. He also is likely to participate as a member of all system-wide instructional and curriculum committees.

Central Office Supervisors or Consultants

Most of the larger school districts provide for a central office staff of supervisors or consultants. These persons possess professional training, substantial experience in teaching, special skills in group process, significant knowledge of instructional materials and methods, and the ability to carry out various kinds of educational research. Some of them may work as general supervisors and some may function as special subject supervisors.

General supervisors. General supervision in the elementary school appeared very early in America. Only since the 1930's has the general supervisor been found in the secondary schools to any extent.

The general supervisor tends to be specialized according to educational levels rather than by subject. Thus the generalist may be assigned as supervisor of the primary, upper elementary, junior high, or senior high levels. General supervisors at all levels, however, tend to fulfill several basic functions:

1. The general supervisor cooperates with the principal to identify instructional problems and to discover promising ways of attacking them. While working in the school building, he operates under the direction of

the principal. He makes the resources of the central supervisory office available to help with the problems and concerns of the local staff. He works with individual teachers only with the approval of the principal. Actually, in a sense he may duplicate the services of the building principal who is expected to work with his staff as a general supervisor. This occasionally may lead to conflict; yet because of competing administrative demands, the principal finds it difficult, if not impossible, to engage in significant supervision without a good deal of assistance.

2. The general supervisor emphasizes the coordinating function. He seeks to bring together interested teachers in order to solve problems. He offers expert help to teachers who can make important contributions for instructional improvement, and he coordinates their efforts.

3. The productive general supervisor makes his group process skills available. He is able to assist groups in the efficient and satisfying identification, attack, and solution of problems. He provides help to committees in order to facilitate their work. He strives to remove blocks which impede progress, attempts to produce group situations which release the potentialities of participants, and encourages leadership which comes from within the group and which may make the group more able to operate efficiently.

4. The central office supervisor constantly works to locate information regarding classroom experimentation, new educational materials, and promising practices. He then makes these available to interested principals and teachers. This requires continuing study, professional reading, and attendance at conventions and workshops of professional associations. Supervisors remain alert to examples of new instructional techniques, interesting uses of teaching media, and action research to be found in the system. They may write up instructional newsletters or memos which describe these developments in order to share this information and to provide recognition for the persons involved.

5. The general supervisor provides production techniques and skills for the benefit of teachers in preparing, editing, duplicating, and distributing courses of study, resource units, and other instructional materials. The task of summarizing and reporting minutes of meetings, lists of recommendations, and progress in terminal reports often falls to the supervisor. In this way he is able to make an important contribution to the continuity and satisfaction of committee work as well as relieving heavily burdened teachers.

6. Administrative functions are increasingly being minimized and reduced in order to enhance the effectiveness of the general supervisor. Teachers will respond differently, most supervisors judge more favorably, to supervision by a person who has little or no administrative authority over them as compared to one who, for example, rates them for tenure or merit raises. Some general supervisors, however, are required to visit teachers for the purpose of rating them and are involved in the hiring

and firing of instructional personnel. Other administrative responsibilities sometimes include the approval of textbook requisitions, consultation regarding promotions and transfers, scheduling of teacher intervisitation, assignment of new teachers to schools in the system, workshop planning and direction, and administration of the assignment of student teachers in the schools.

Special supervisors. Special supervisors initially were used as itinerant teachers when a number of special subjects were added to the curriculum in the late 1800's. They were employed because of their knowledge of the subject. Most teachers and principals admittedly knew very little about art and music. Therefore, the special supervisor or special teacher at first taught the subject himself and later assisted the regular teachers to gain some minimal competence so they could teach it themselves.

Today it is possible to find central office supervisors of all the subject areas as well as other specialities such as reading, spelling, writing, driver education, and special education. Few school systems which are committed to special supervision can afford to employ full time supervisors or consultants in every possible speciality. Instead, they tend to hire persons to supervise areas which seem to need the most improvement or to supervise those subjects which are judged to be most basic.

The special supervisor attached to the central office operates much like the general supervisor except that he tends to be called upon more as a resource in his content speciality rather than for his ability to coordinate and facilitate group action. The special supervisor must possess expertness in the subject matter in which he specializes and in the methods of teaching it. For example, he may make important contributions in developing vertical articulation. A language arts supervisor may work with teachers in grades one through twelve in order to secure smoother flow of content and less unnecessary duplication in the teaching of English through the grades. He might assist a committee of representative teachers to develop a K-12 curriculum outline of subject matter in English. He, of course, will need to be up-to-date in regard to new materials and emerging trends in the teaching of his subject. As an accomplished teacher the special supervisor may do some demonstration teaching, especially in helping beginning teachers. He often participates in in-service training activities and may establish and maintain a library of resource units, curriculum guides, pertinent readings, and instructional materials for the benefit of teachers in his special area of interest. Sometimes outside consultants are invited by the special supervisor to meet with interested instructional personnel. His most signal contributions tend to come through his expertness in the subject and his overall perspective of this area of the curriculum.

General versus special supervision. There seems to be no general agreement as to which approach is clearly superior—general supervision or special supervision. Each has its advantages and disadvantages.

Today's recognition of the values of correlation and integration of different subjects seems to point up an advantage of general supervision. The general supervisor is able to bring together teachers of various subjects to explore the possibilities of such relationships. He seeks to intensify horizontal articulation. The special supervisor, on the other hand, is more likely to accomplish equally vital progress toward vertical articulation within his subject area.

The general supervisor approaches the problem of improving instruction much as the principal does. Neither can be equally expert in all subjects; thus they work most productively along the lines of coordinating the efforts of interested educational workers and then supplying resources, both material and personnel, to help in their work. The principal in his relations with supervisors is much more likely to accept the recommendations of the specialist than of the generalist. The special supervisor presumably is better equipped by training and experience to offer specific and knowledgeable opinions in regard to his content area.

Special supervision, while it presents the real advantage of expert assistance, may result in increasing the compartmentalization of subjects. High school teachers, especially, because of training and departmental organization of the school, naturally tend to form close attachments with teachers of the same subject area and may display little interest or understanding of the needs and concerns of teachers of other subjects. The special supervisor, in working to develop strong identification and participation in improvement programs in a particular subject area, may inadvertently foster more curricular myopia.

Balance in curricular improvement activity may be difficult to achieve in a system which has special supervisors in only a few areas. Experience has shown that an enthusiastic special supervisor often is able to generate a great deal of interest, set in motion a variety of activities, and secure a disproportionate share of attention to his subject speciality. Other curricular areas which rely on the part-time supervisory efforts of building principals are not likely to keep pace. A general supervisor may be able to distribute his time and energies more evenly among the interested personnel in all areas needing improvement.

At the elementary school level teachers sometimes report the unhappy experience of being caught in the middle of conflicting pressures from helpful special supervisors. Each special supervisor attempts to promote the teaching of his speciality, often without recognizing that his great interest and concern is only one of the subjects with which the elementary teacher must deal.

Generally, the weight of evidence would seem to favor general supervision over special supervision. However, a sort of compromise approach may be found in some systems. The general supervisor theoretically is qualified to provide assistance to all subjects within the educational segment to which he is assigned. In practice, however, each general supervisor may be encouraged to develop expertness in at least two subject areas. For example, a general supervisor for elementary education might possess special competence and interest in reading and arithmetic or in handwriting and elementary science, in addition to a broad knowledge and experience in teaching in these grades. Such a person can embody many of the best features of both supervisory approaches.

Supervisors attached to the central office often seem inevitably trapped by the contradictions of their role in the school system. The supervisor realizes the central importance of the classroom teacher to improved instruction. The individual teacher must change if learning and teaching in his classroom are to change; yet the central office supervisor may be denied significant face-to-face contacts with teachers because of reluctant or overworked building principals. The supervisor knows that his best chance for success lies in a consultative approach without line authority. Teachers will develop more democratic ways of working with the supervisor if he does not have the administrative responsibility of rating them for tenure or promotion. Groups will seek his help because of his demonstrated ability to help them achieve their goals rather than because of his authority over them. Principals are apt to work cooperatively with the supervisor if they do not have to compete with him for the allegiance of their teachers; yet a continuing frustration for supervisors is that sometimes it appears that certain blocks to progress exist which might be removed with a little authority. The supervisor may identify serious instructional inadequacies which need immediate correction. He knows, however, that the best results come from a slow, deliberate approach which attempts to awaken teacher understanding of the problem, to stimulate the desire to do something constructive about it, and to initiate procedures which promise improvement.

CHAPTER III

Responsibilities of Supervisory Personnel in a School

In recent years American public education has been characterized by the steadily increasing size of school systems. This increase is the result of such developments as consolidation and unification of school units, urbanization, and population growth. This dramatic change became the focus of much attention, for it brought constant problems of adjusting and reorganizing to handle larger and more complex administrative units. Population explosions in some locations in the far West and Southwest, for example, required system-level planning and organization to meet the unprecedented demand for educational services. School superintendents, as an aspect of this attention to system-wide organization, worked to explore and solve problems of providing central office supervision. At the same time, however, the strong feeling persisted that the building unit itself provided a most productive setting for instructional change.

The individual school possesses an essential characteristic which enhances and unifies supervisory efforts. It has an obvious organismic wholeness [1] which is supported by the community structure within which it exists. In the perception of parents, change in the schools has to do with the local school which their children attend. Generally, the contributions of lay persons are most helpful and constructive if made at the local school level. The individual school has cohesiveness because of the natural unity of its educational staff, student body, and the building within which it operates. This organismic wholeness may result in an institutional personality which sometimes has a profound effect upon the program of the school. Within the same school system different schools are observed to have substantially different traditions, attitudes toward the proper role

---

[1] John I. Goodlad, "The Individual School and its Principal: Key Setting and Key Person in Educational Leadership," *Educational Leadership*, Vol. 13 (October, 1955), 2–3.

of the school, and approaches to instructional improvement. Thus supervisory efforts may take different forms in schools within the same district.

The individual school, as a productive setting for change, has the advantage of regular face-to-face relationships among its personnel. Central office personnel, on the other hand, must spread their attention and efforts among many different schools and many different problems. It is more difficult for them to identify with and become a real part of local problem situations. The improvements, of course, ultimately are realized in the classroom itself; yet relatively few teachers have the resources, training, and self-sufficiency to make outstanding progress by themselves. The individual school unit, therefore, deserves recognition as a vital context for supervision.

The Small High School

The small high school embodies a number of characteristics which may facilitate or inhibit improvement of learning and teaching. An obvious advantage is the small, and often close-knit, educational staff. Teachers regularly operate as a committee of the whole, facing together the pressing problems of curriculum and instruction. This procedure in a group of manageable size facilitates a unified improvement activity. The close working relationships enable teachers to secure a good understanding of the total school program and to develop their subject areas into an essential part of the broad services of the school. Instructional problems which affect the entire curriculum are more easily perceived, explored, and dealt with by the staff. The principal, as educational leader, is close to his faculty and generally is in a good position to sense emerging problems and concerns.

The factor of size, however, has disadvantages. Teachers sometimes must teach in several areas; thus their interest and energy may be divided. A small staff may have limited resources represented among its personnel. For example, the group is less likely to find a person with great facility in group process, specialized skills in educational research, or outstanding ability in the production of resource units, course outlines, teaching guides, and reports. Teachers who possess strong personalities may occasionally dominate a small group or unduly influence faculty judgments. Small high schools are especially subject to the problem of short teacher tenure. Teachers, like Americans in general, have become increasingly mobile. This is usually a problem; but the small high school, in rural areas especially, may have to replace one-fourth to one-half or even more of its faculty each year as teachers use the rural school system as a stepping stone to employment in a larger high school in a more attractive geographical location. The constant turnover makes sustained improvement difficult if not impossible.

The small secondary school makes heavy demands upon its administrative head. He must administer the school usually without much assistance from the superintendent's office, if there is one, and often without substantial help in his individual school. Principals in very small high schools commonly teach a class or two; clerical help is often part-time or inadequately trained; and multiple responsibilities urgently require attention. Moreover, the administrator himself may possess only minimum preparation and limited experience.

The improvement of instruction, of course, is just as important in a small high school as in a large one. Even though the organization for supervision is likely to be fairly simple and direct, several different persons may perform responsible roles.

The principal. The administrative head must fulfill a crucial role in supervision. The realistic principal of the small high school recognizes that he is the general supervisor of his school. He will need to work directly in supervision, for usually there are no assistants to whom he may delegate a significant portion of this responsibility. He is the chief executive of the individual school and his role requires that he carry both the administrative and supervisory loads. Administrative details often appear more urgent and pressing than supervisory activities; yet, ultimately, the success of both the school and the principal are to be measured in the increasing quality of the instructional program. As a result, the principal of the small high school commonly has the uneasy feeling that he is trying to do everything but should be doing more. This sentiment is well-expressed by one administrator who says:

> My days are usually very full as I try to be principal, educational consultant, guidance director, head custodian, and substitute teacher first class all rolled into one. It becomes all too easy to permit my

educational focus to become blurred and blunted by spreading myself too thin.[2]

It is difficult to separate the tasks performed into categories which are purely supervisory or purely administrative. However, the principal in the small high school commonly engages in various kinds of action which have important implications for supervision.

1. The principal is the official leader and final authority in the building. He works within the policy framework set down by the board of education and the superintendent. He is the pivotal figure in supervision.

As the supervisory leader in his school he must set the stage for instructional improvement activity, support teachers willing to experiment with new and promising practices, and enthusiastically contribute a significant portion of his time and energy to the improvement of learning and teaching. He stimulates teachers through personal example and genuine interest. He attempts to provide sympathetic and knowledgeable guidance. At the same time he attempts to identify and encourage leadership in others of his staff.

The principal's leadership, at least initially, is derived from the authority invested in his position and from teacher expectations of his role. Sustained, productive leadership depends upon the personality of the principal, his concept of supervisory leadership, his desire to supervise, and his ability to apportion his time wisely.

2. In the small high school the principal must coordinate and facilitate the efforts made by his staff. Although he deals with a relatively small group, he must deliberately seek to identify problems and concerns, establish and maintain a free flow of communication among the staff, form committees and groups to deal with instructional problems, search for pertinent resources, and provide the time and opportunity for fruitful work. He needs to plan so that even the mechanics of textbook adoption, purchase of audio-visual aids, supplementary books, and other instructional materials will contribute to teacher improvement and satisfaction. He must use to best advantage central office personnel, county and state consultants, and university assistance when these are available.

3. The principal is expected to know the community within which the school exists, the curricular program offered by his school, the student population enrolled, the professional staff employed, the school plant and equipment, and the guiding policies of the school district. He continually evaluates the instructional program by studying records and test results, through conferences and interviews with parents, students and teachers, and by actual visitation of classes. He is an important resource to his staff because of his perspective and knowledge of the overall situation.

---

[2] Donald E. Hagen, "Big Problems of the Small High School—Potential Assets vs. Size Limitations," *NASSP Bulletin,* Vol. 46 (September, 1962), 51.

Through his active participation he makes his unique contributions available to groups.

4. The principal's personnel responsibilities have great supervisory potential. In the small secondary school he is directly involved in employing teachers and deciding upon whether or not to retain them. The school board may require him to rate them. Usually he handles the orientation of new teachers and provides some special assistance to beginning teachers. He constructs the daily class schedule, so important to job satisfaction and teacher growth. Faculty bulletins and the teachers' handbook are also the result of the principal's labors.

Almost universally the principal of the small high school is responsible for whatever supervision that takes place in his school. Unless he is able to initiate action, nurture, and sustain it, very little instructional improvement is likely to occur.

Deans.   Some slightly larger high schools have deans or advisors for the students. Professional persons in these positions may be delegated responsibility for working with students in matters of attendance, morale, extra-curricular functions, and minor discipline problems. They often contribute to supervision by assisting teachers to know and understand their students better. They are utilized by committees and groups as resources in the solution of problems which require detailed knowledge of the school's pupil population.

Supervising or consulting teachers.   The introduction and development of the master teacher plan [3] which has proved so successful in the elementary school has its counterpart in the high school supervising or consulting teacher. This position normally is filled by an experienced teacher already on the staff, a person who is noted for his fine teaching and for his outstanding ability to work with other faculty members. In the small high school he would be released from all or part of his teaching load and be expected to act in a consultative capacity to the rest of the staff. The supervising teacher commonly is appointed for one or at the most two years whereupon he returns to full-time teaching. He offers help and guidance especially to the less experienced teachers and those new to the school. The great advantage, of course, is that teachers are usually more inclined to seek his help, ask his advice, and invite him to visit their classes, for he obviously is not an administrator who may have to rate them for retention, salary, or promotion purposes. Instead, he

---

[3] See, for example, Helen L. Quinn, "Developing a Program for the Master Teacher," *Chicago Schools Journal,* Vol. 38 (September-October, 1956), 23–28.

is a fellow teacher, recognized for his ability to provide assistance and given some time to help them. Some attempt, of course, is made to select supervising teachers who possess special competence in various subject areas, although during their time of tenure each operates as a general supervisor to the whole high school faculty. This position, which seems to have promise for the small junior or senior high school, represents a modest attempt to provide supervisory services of a nonadministrative nature to augment the sometimes limited efforts of the principal.

A variation of this plan is emerging in schools of various sizes which utilize team teaching. A master teacher is chosen to head up the instructional team and provide some supervision for his team mates.

The Large High School

The very large high school naturally presents complex problems of management and supervision. The professional staff is large and varied. Problems of communication and organization for effective effort are compounded. More personnel necessarily are engaged in the large tasks of administering and supervising. Face-to-face relationships between the head administrator and the teachers become less frequent and more formal. Individual classroom teachers find it difficult to achieve and maintain perspective of their activities as an integral part of the total program of the school. The faculty tends to become a loose confederation of departments or groups of teachers, each organized by common subject-matter interests or similar responsibilities. The evolving power structure of the staff and the negotiation of differences between groups, each of which views the instructional program from a special frame of reference, may become important factors in school-wide decisions. Scheduling of classes, assignment of rooms, and routine arrangements are likely to be accomplished impersonally without consideration of the individual differences and preferences of the teachers involved.

The large school, however, is likely to possess many resources. The finances of a large unit may permit the employment of well-trained and experienced assistants to the principal, who also is more likely to be well-qualified for his position. Significant help may be available from the superintendent's office. A variety of instructional aids and materials may be present. To utilize these resources and materials and to provide the multiple supervisory services needed, a number of different persons bear various responsibilities.

The principal. Principals in large secondary schools have long taken two points of view in regard to their role in supervision.[4] Although there is no question that principals are the executive heads of the school, responsible for all aspects of its operation, there are some differing opinions regarding their place in supervision. One point of view holds that the management responsibilities are so numerous and pressing that the high school principal cannot realistically engage in genuine supervision. In very small high schools the administrative head must supervise. In the very large high school, however, the principal necessarily is engrossed in the general administration of this large and complex organization and has neither the time nor the opportunity to supervise instruction. The second point of view asserts that the principal inevitably operates as the coordinating director of the supervisory services. He may carry out this coordination poorly or well; yet, as part of his general management of the school, he does actually engage in supervision. His grasp of the overall picture, his knowledge of long-range trends and directions of desired change, and his insight into school policies help qualify him to accept this necessary task.

The real difference in these two positions seems to hang upon varying definitions of supervision. If one conceives of supervision as including anything which contributes to improved learning and teaching, the principal in the large high school does indeed have real and tangible responsibilities in supervision. True, he may not be able to engage directly in classroom visitation and individual teacher conferences to any substantial extent, but his contributions to supervision are still vital. In the very large secondary school he probably operates more nearly like the system superintendent who emphasizes coordination and organization of supervisory services than like the small high school principal who acts directly as general supervisor.

The principal, of course, must work to establish a favorable atmosphere for instructional improvement in his school. He hopes that the enthusiasm and interest which he displays will prove contagious and will impel the professional staff to seek positive change.

---

[4] See, for example, Theodore D. Rice, "Supervisory Personnel: The Principal," *NASSP Bulletin,* Vol. 34 (December, 1950), 30–31.

Beyond this he seeks to organize the teachers and educational workers and to facilitate supervisory effort. Responsibilities are clearly defined and intraschool working relationships are clarified. The role and contributions of outside consultants are explained. The principal organizes the teachers into departments and/or committees. He may provide for a representative cabinet or advisory council to consider with him problems which affect the school, thus making it possible for groups of concerned teachers to deal with the problems.

The principal fosters instructional improvement by supporting experimentation in his school. He recognizes that promising practices occasionally fail and that evaluation may show the new procedure to be less effective than the old. He knows the resources of the central staff and outside agencies, and he invites their participation at appropriate points. The head administrator strives to open channels of communication so that pressing concerns of individual classroom teachers may come to the attention of supervisory persons. He may be able to schedule the teachers of a certain subject area to a common planning period so that they may attack an instruction problem. In these and similar ways he accepts his responsibility to facilitate the improvement of learning and teaching. Thus the principal of the large high school contributes most significantly to the supervisory program by nurturing a favorable atmosphere, mobilizing resources, organizing personnel, and facilitating desired change.

The assistant principal. The sizable high school commonly employs one or more assistant principals. The position has developed somewhat haphazardly over the years; yet current trends indicate a tendency to reduce purely clerical and routine duties, to conceive the operation of the principal and his assistants as an administrative team, and to increase the assistant principals' responsibilities for significant administrative and supervisory functions. The assistant principal is likely to be charged with major or shared responsibilities in such broad areas as pupil accounting, school control, extracurricular activities, and curriculum.

Obviously an assistant principal who works directly with the pupils and their activities may contribute to supervision through his intimate understanding of the student population. He is in a position to help evaluate the instructional program, to identify emerging instructional problems and weak spots, and to assist teachers to better understand their pupils. He is likely to be used as a resource by committees and groups at work on instructional problems.

The assistant principal who deals directly with the curriculum [5] works as a general supervisor in the high school under the direction of the principal. He is commonly delegated major supervisory responsibilities for upgrading the quality of learning and teaching. His approaches and functions approximate those of any general supervisor working within a school unit.

Some very large high schools have adopted the grade principal or "school-within-a-school" plan. In this plan a professionally trained person of assistant principal rank is placed in charge of the teachers, students, instructional program, and facilities of one grade level of the high school. This person works to direct and coordinate the activities of his assigned grade. This arrangement seems to embody many of the advantages and disadvantages of the principal in the small high school.

The coordinator of instruction.   Many large high schools have moved in the direction of providing a clearer division between administrative and supervisory responsibilities. While the assistant principal clearly occupies a place in the chain of command, the title and conception of the coordinator of instruction is more nearly that of a staff official.

The coordinator of instruction may rank with or slightly below an assistant principal in the organization, and he is the person to whom the major responsibility for supervision in the school is delegated. It is his job to strive for instructional improvement. This position is ideally filled by a person who possesses superior qualities of supervisory leadership and coordination. It is less likely to be considered an internship for someone interested in becoming a principal at a later date.

The broad function of the coordinator is that of general supervision in the high school. He normally is responsible for the work of other supervisory personnel. For example, the department heads work with him in the special supervision of their academic departments. He seeks to stimulate and assist the teachers in their study of problems of instruction; he knows and utilizes available resources

---

[5] For a description of typical duties, see Gareth B. Goddard, "The Assistant Principal—Understudy or Partner in Professional Leadership," *NASSP Bulletin,* Vol. 46 (September, 1962), 33.

to help in problem solution; and he applies his skills of group process to make the work of committees and groups more effective. The principal remains the executive head of the school but he concentrates the supervision in one person, the coordinator of instruction.

The department head. The department head or chairman has long been a part of the organization of large high schools; yet in practice this position has seldom lived up to its supervisory potential. Often the department head receives the job (through appointment by the principal or by departmental election) as a reward for long and dedicated service to the school rather than for outstanding qualities of leadership and teaching excellence. The position has commonly included a heavy load of routine clerical and administrative responsibilities and insufficient release from teaching; therefore, no significant supervision is accomplished.

Ideally the head of the department works as a part-time special supervisor to the teachers in his academic subject area. In large high schools the department head commonly handles the orientation of new teachers and works to help inexperienced teachers gain confidence and increasing competence. Within the limits of time available (typically his teaching load is reduced by one or two classes), he assists any instructor who perceives the need for improvement. Through conferences and meetings he helps the teachers keep abreast of new developments in materials, methods, and content. He promotes continuing teacher growth by working with the administration to arrange in-service education such as workshops, demonstrations, and discussions. He holds regular departmental meetings to evaluate the program, explore problems, share ideas, and develop group identity.

An important facet of the department head's role is to maintain two-way communication channels between the administration and the classroom teachers in his department. He represents the interests of the department in serving on the principal's advisory council and school committees. He communicates and interprets school policies and decisions to his teachers and brings their concerns, feelings, needs, and proposals to the attention of the top administrative level in the school.

Given a person who possesses real leadership abilities and teaching competence, reduction of many of the clerical duties now associated with the role, increased time and opportunity for supervision, and provision for coordinating instructional improvement among different departments, the position of department head is more likely to realize its potential.

The Elementary School

The elementary school tends to differ from the high school in a number of essential characteristics which have implications for supervision. Teachers generally differ in education and in the nature and conditions of teaching assignments. The secondary school teacher is a subject-matter specialist by training, assignment, and inclination. The majority of elementary teachers are generalists. In the lower grades especially, they are prepared to guide students in the wide range of experiences met in the school day. Some elementary schools employ special teachers in certain subjects such as music, art, physical education, and foreign languages. These persons, however, often work as itinerant teachers, moving about among the schools in the district and sometimes operating as special consultants to the regular teachers. High school teachers commonly deal with a different group of youngsters each period of the day, while elementary teachers ordinarily are responsible for the same pupils all, or at least half, of the school day. Secondary school faculty members tend to feel responsible and directly concerned with only one aspect of the total curriculum—their special subject field. The teacher in the elementary school is more likely to understand and to feel committed to the total instructional program.

The large high school is likely to be organized into departments or academic divisions with consequent lack of unity in the staff. Administrative personnel are expected to accept responsibility for dealing with problems of counseling, attendance, student morale, extracurricular activities, and the like. In the elementary school, teachers are commonly placed in charge of a room which is largely self-sufficient. They are responsible for instruction, counseling, and social control under the overall direction of the principal. As a result elementary education has developed more teacher feeling of responsibility for the total curricular program and generally a more democratic school organization.

The principal.   At the elementary school level the principal has long operated more effectively in instructional supervision than at the high school level. School building units are generally of more manageable size and are usually less complicated. Elementary schools have fewer extracurricular activities with which to deal. For example, the principal is not tempted to fall into an expedient preoccupation with the scheduling of interscholastic athletics, choosing basketball and football officials, or managing regional and sectional playoffs.

The elementary school principal, like all principals, is the executive head of the school and is in charge of the wide range of administrative and supervisory responsibilities. He is apt to be considered the general supervisor of his school. Unless he is the victim of a school system policy (which sometimes places a promising young administrator in the elementary school principalship even though his training and experience have been in high schools in order to groom him for a high position in the office of the superintendent), the elementary principal is likely to have extended and notable teaching experience at the elementary school level. Thus he has a pertinent background of training and experience from which to supervise. High school principals, of course, find it impossible to develop expertness in all subject areas and, as a consequence, are reluctant to offer assistance to teachers in many specialities. The elementary principal, on the other hand, generally is able to discuss instructional difficulties with all of his teachers and to offer positive and helpful suggestions and assistance. With the advantage of less complicated administrative demands, he is more likely to visit classes, confer with teachers, and directly offer help.

The elementary principal often prefers to work democratically as a process person or discussion leader. Teachers are brought together to initiate problems, to analyze and discuss them, and to propose ways of attempting their solution. The principal's attitude toward progress in curriculum improvement, his interpretation of the policies of the superintendent and school board, his knowledge of the community, and his support of teacher experimentation are powerful influences in the actions taken to upgrade learning and teaching in his school. In the elementary school, however, he deals with a group of teachers who are apt to be concerned with the broad range of curricular experiences offered and the total growth of each youngster. In this context he is less plagued by the tugging and pulling of various subject groups, each of which seeks to gain some advantage for its area. The principal seeks to coordinate and organize his staff for the solution of problems, to assist them to secure the resources needed to accomplish their goals, and to encourage them to complete the tasks. He must know and utilize central office consultants in cooperative supervision. The principal may discover resources in other elementary schools within the school system, educational personnel with special competencies in the county or state offices, and helpful college and university consultants which he can bring into the activities of his staff.

The nonteaching elementary principal is in a strategic position to evaluate constantly the instructional program of his school. He deals with the school records; he organizes and directs the testing program; he has the opportunity to observe the varied activities within his school; he talks with parents and students; and he meets with secondary administrators in order to appraise the instructional services of his school. This broad view complements the more limited evaluation of the program by the teachers. As part of his supervisory responsibilities, the principal contributes to the identification of areas in need of work and to the evaluation of attempts at improvement.

The elementary principal has close and direct responsibilities for the personnel in his school. He commonly has an important voice in the employment and retention of teachers. He controls the assignment and reassignment of instructors to various grade levels. This is, of course, important for the teaching satisfaction and effectiveness. It may have great significance for supervision when, under the widely prevalent self-contained classroom organization, he is able to secure a well-balanced staff which includes teachers who have expertness and interest in various special areas in addition to their basic preparation. Thus he may provide a situation wherein teachers can find special help within their own faculty.

In elementary schools the principal typically carries the supervisory load, although occasionally he may have assistants to help him.

The building consultant—resource or helping teacher. The instructional consultant who works within a single school may be called a helping teacher, master teacher, or resource teacher. These educational personnel are released from all or part of their teaching load in order to work as consultants to the faculty. They are chosen from among the professional staff because they have demonstrated superior teaching ability, are known to possess great understanding of children, and have a sound grasp of the crucial elements which provide an exemplary learning-teaching situation. They have the ability to cooperate with others and are inclined to seek personal satisfaction in the success and improvement of their colleagues. These consultants serve temporarily as supervisors under the direction of the principal and return to full-time teaching upon completion of their tenure in this position. They are clearly fellow teachers who are freed from teaching duties in order to assist the faculty in instructional improvement.

The building consultant's productivity largely depends upon his own personality and approach, his demonstrated ability to provide substantial assistance, the attitudes of fellow faculty members toward the position, and the direction and support provided by the principal. His duties are many and varied.[6]

One of his main responsibilities is the inexperienced teacher. Orientation to the school and direct help are provided. The consultant assists in the difficult task of planning and organizing the teacher's work. Advice on teaching materials and learning aids is provided. When appropriate, the consultant prepares and executes demonstration lessons and plans for a detailed discussion afterward. Beginning instructors often ask for ideas in improving class participation and classroom control. Sometimes assistance is needed in suggesting ways of continuing professional growth.

The consultant also works with more experienced teachers in improving instruction. If the building consultant is acknowledged to be an outstanding teacher, the regular staff will welcome classroom visitation and will cooperatively explore ways to approach mutual problems. The building consultant has the advantage of working in one school and feels a responsibility and identification with the problems discovered. Both the classroom teacher and the supervisor are a part of the problem situation and are likely to feel committed to find a solution. Consultants often assist in the evaluation of learning. They sometimes even take the experienced teachers' classes so that they can do special planning, work as a team in

---

[6] A description of one teacher's experience is given in Zoralyn V. Salario, "The Role of the Master Teacher is a Varied One," *Chicago Schools Bulletin,* Vol. 38 (September-October, 1956), 29–31.

dealing with special problem groups, prepare curricular materials, and facilitate the sharing of ideas.

The building consultant is given the opportunity to explore new instructional materials and teaching aids and to secure them for examination by the faculty. He obtains descriptions and results of action research and experimentation which seem pertinent, and he may arrange for the purchase of needed books and pamphlets for the faculty reading shelf. He sometimes arranges for teacher inter-visitation, workshops, discussions, faculty meetings, and other in-service activities.

The function of the building consultant, in short, is to expand and extend the supervisory services offered by the school principal. Moreover, the contributions are made by a person who is clearly a fellow teacher and whose authority is earned mainly through demonstrated competence and understanding of the local situation.

Schools Use Central Office Consultants

Many individual schools have the opportunity to use central office supervisory personnel. As part of a large district they must share these resources with the other schools. The individual school, however, may or may not utilize the central office supervisors and consultants wisely, depending on how well the principal and his educational staff understand the nature of productive relationships and the potential values which may be realized.

The modern concept of supervision recognizes that consultants from the central office must work with and through the principal of the elementary or secondary school. The principal is the administrative and supervisory head of his school and gears overall responsibility for its operation. The consultant offers supervisory services, but it is the principal's decision whether or not to make use of these resources at appropriate points. In practice, the central office person enters the building at the pleasure of the principal and while there works under his direction.

Cooperative relationships are sought among the people involved in instructional improvement. The classroom teacher is the elemental agent in the process of change. Only as he changes will classroom practice be improved. The central office supervisor brings special resources such as knowledge of group dynamics, production skills and facilities, and sources of information not available to the local building staff. The principal possesses pertinent knowledge and understanding of the local situation such as nature of the community, student population, professional staff, and the instructional program of the school. The team—consisting of principal, supervisor, and teacher—share the responsibility for effecting instructional improvement and cooperatively work toward its achievement.

The central office consultant is limited in his contributions because he necessarily must spread his energies and resources among many schools in the system. He probably lacks intimate insight into the nature of the individual school's student population, the strengths and weaknesses of the faculty, close and continuing acquaintance with the building and equipment, evolving local modes of operation, shifting patterns of interrelationships among the staff, and prevalent feelings and attitudes toward change. At the same time, he is apt to have a broad view of the total program of the school system. He can safeguard the individual school from excessive provincialism. His function may be to bring new perspective to local problems, to suggest different points of view, to help broaden the vision of building personnel, and to indicate new possibilities.

Ideally, the central office consultant works in a staff capacity. He has little or no administrative authority. For example, his services are better received and evaluated if he is not required to rate teachers. He ordinarily does not visit classes unless invited. As a supervisory consultant he must convince teachers of the worth of his suggestions. The special art of supervision is the ability to help teachers discover better approaches to instruction, rather than directing or requiring them to use different methods or teaching materials.

CHAPTER IV

Qualifications of Supervisors

The real focus of the work of supervision must inevitably rest upon people rather than upon things. Success in supervision is achieved only through the changes in behavior of educational personnel which result in improved learning and teaching in the classroom. The supervisor works indirectly to gain the desired end. This is the source of considerable and persistent frustration, for a great many supervisors have been outstanding performers in the classroom. As supervisory workers, however, they must accept the fact that their contributions are achieved through their ability to induce, encourage, and facilitate progress mainly without the use of administrative authority, or sometimes in spite of it.

With increased insight into the benefits of democratic and creative approaches to supervision, the autocratic and dictatorial procedures of old are seen to be inappropriate and ineffective for genuine and lasting progress. It may seem more efficient in time simply to require teachers to use a new method or teaching procedure. This method, however, is less effective in lasting results. Success in supervision lies in changing teacher attitudes and understandings which, in turn, may result in changed behavior. Accordingly, the nature of educational leadership has been described as "that action or behavior among individuals and groups which causes both the individual and the groups to move toward educational goals that are increasingly mutually acceptable to them." [1] The successful supervisor must possess a combination of personal and professional characteristics which will fit such a conception of democratic leadership.

---

[1] *Leadership for Improving Instruction,* 1960 Yearbook (Washington, D.C.: Association for Supervision and Curriculum Development, National Education Association, 1960), p. 27.

Personal Characteristics

In choosing persons who are likely to fulfill the role expectations of the modern supervisor, the following personal characteristics seem to be essential.

Ability to win respect and confidence. The full-time supervisor normally works with teachers in a staff relationship, rather than a line-authority relationship. Therefore, his ability to earn the respect of co-workers is crucial in such a role. His demonstrated competence, integrity, and respect for the individuality of others will go far to secure the confidence of colleagues.

Empathy and sensitivity. The work of supervision is carried on within complex interrelationships. The quality of empathy and its concomitant sensitivity to the feelings and reactions of others are crucial to successful leadership. The insensitive person will not become a successful teacher, for, lacking insight into the responses of his students to their experiences in the classroom, he must necessarily follow a mechanical approach to teaching. The insensitive supervisor may misread the motives and reactions of associates and thus may not work toward positive change in teacher attitudes, which will subsequently be reflected in changed instructional performance.

Enthusiasm. People who work constantly with others in a leadership role recognize the important factor of momentum. After the processes are set in motion, they must be sustained. The personal enthusiasm of the supervisor is important to the continuation of momentum. Moreover, the quality of enthusiasm is often contagious, and others may then help in carrying the work to completion.

Feeling of adequacy. The successful supervisor is likely to be optimistic, self-confident, and persistent in the face of adversity. In spite of uncooperative administrators and overburdened teachers, he may continue to seek and find productive ways of working. He has developed a positive view of his own abilities and limitations. In order to achieve a feeling of adequacy, "people need to have accurate, realistic, non-defensive concepts of self." [2]

---

[2] *Perceiving Behaving Becoming,* 1962 Yearbook (Washington, D.C.: Association for Supervision and Curriculum Development, National Education Association, 1962), p. 119.

Originality. People in education, as in many other occupations, seem always to be seeking to answer the same old questions and coming up with the same old answers. Educational leadership should seek fresh points of view and new questions to pose. Part of the great contribution of the original and creative supervisor is to pry teachers loose from established, comfortable approaches which leave something to be desired and to give them potentially more productive alternatives. If it is true, according to Earl C. Kelley, Carl R. Rogers, A. H. Maslow, and Arthur W. Combs,[3] that there is the capacity for creativity and originality within all humans, then an aspect of the task of supervision is to remove some of the blocks to its development and to release this potential in others. The supervisor may foster creativity through personal example and through the establishment of a climate which supports and prizes originality.

Sense of humor. The quality of the supervisor's relationships with others is often conditioned by his sense of humor. People are more likely to accept and respond well to constructive criticism if it is made within a pleasant atmosphere. Most human relationships are more likely to grow and flourish in a situation characterized by warmth and informality than in continual deadly seriousness. For this reason the person who would be a supervisor should cultivate this characteristic.

Sense of relative value. Supervision commonly involves a wide variety of problems and needs. Many of these are fleeting and temporary; others are of great import to long range improvement. Accordingly, the supervisor must have a sense of proportion and perspective. He must be able to assess the relative value of educational aims and ways of working. He must keep the overall view of long-range progress in mind. He recognizes that all educational workers, including himself, have a limited amount of energy to expend. Moreover, many demands from home and family, from personal interests, from society, and from the school legitimately press upon this energy potential. He must attempt to utilize the available energies to best advantage in the light of long-term results.

Sincerity. The sincere supervisor is marked by his commitment to the task of instructional improvement, his integrity in dealing with others, and his respect for the individuality of co-workers. If

---

[3] *Ibid.*, p. 142–43.

teachers are convinced that the supervisor is sincerely working toward the gradual improvement of learning and teaching in their school, not because of some personal motive, they are more likely to participate fully in the cooperative solution of mutual problems. Successful long-range group efforts are characterized by sincerity and dedication among all those concerned. Insincerity on the part of the official leader is almost certain to undermine the group's capacity for productive work.

Resourcefulness. The supervisor needs outstanding resources of intelligence, training, and experience. Educational personnel look to him for assistance when they have exhausted the familiar and the obvious. He must be resourceful in finding new ways of working, tapping new sources of assistance, and suggesting alternative procedures to try. Part of the essential concept of the supervisor's role hangs upon this desired quality of resourcefulness. Much of the advanced training and the extended and successful experience sought in prospective supervisors is considered important because it enables him to make contributions to the efforts of the staff to improve in its work.

Professional Qualifications

Supervision is carried on by a number of different persons in and outside the local organization of the schools. Some work within the individual school itself; some offer assistance from the central office of the school system; and some make contributions as members of outside agencies such as the office of the county superintendent of schools, the state department of education, and colleges and universities. Supervision may be accomplished by official leaders, such as principals and superintendents, who are given line administrative authority. These services may be performed by educational workers who bear the titles of supervisors, coordinators, or consultants and who work in a position of staff status. Some persons work part-time and some full-time in supervision. Thus it is difficult to specify a set of professional qualifications which would be appropriate to all. The full-time supervisor working within a school unit, however, would seem to need the following professional training, experiences, and attributes if he would develop the varied competencies demanded by such a position.

Broad general education. It is generally agreed that the supervisor should be broadly educated. For example, a report of a national conference of professors of educational administration called for a broad general education and asserted: "The educational leader's effectiveness will undoubtedly be conditioned by his breadth and depth of understanding of human beings and social phenomena." [4] The person who would lead in instructional improvement needs to secure a foundational understanding of the humanities, the sciences, and the social sciences. He ought to have experience with and appreciation of the fine and practical arts. He must know and prize the American democratic society within which he lives.

This broad base in general education is calculated to help him become a liberally educated person—one who has explored and has a feeling for a variety of subject areas, one who possesses a wide range of interests, and one who has the basis for understanding and communicating with other persons of diverse backgrounds in the schools and in the community. The general education should provide him with sound communication skills, the basic tools of his work.

Professional education. The professional education of the supervisor begins with his undergraduate preservice education to become an elementary or secondary teacher. During this phase of his training he must have developed substantial expertness in the subjects which he teaches. In addition he will have:

1. Secured an understanding of the growth and development of children and youth;
2. Gained insight into the processes by which learning and teaching take place;
3. Developed a concept of the role of the elementary or secondary teacher in public education;
4. Become acquainted with the characteristics and functions of public education today;
5. Explored a variety of teaching techniques and materials which have proved themselves in the classroom;
6. Mastered a number of guiding principles which provide the basis for adapting, refining, and developing teaching approaches;
7. Demonstrated competence through actual student teaching experiences.

---

[4] *Educational Leaders—Their Function and Preparation* (New York: Division of Educational Administration, Teachers College, Columbia University, 1948), p. 36.

Subsequent professional education to at least a master's degree is expected. Recommended areas of study, derived through the analysis of research, application of logic, and a three-year study of successful practices in the education of supervisors by the Southern States Work Conference, include:

> *A supervision core.* Some study and practice should be had in administration, supervision, personality development, leadership or the group processes, and general curriculum—elementary and secondary.
> *Specialized curriculum areas.* The general instructional supervisor should be able to work with confidence in at least the areas of human growth and development, reading, the arts, and the social issues. Special supervisors should develop particular skill in their own area of specialization.[5]

In addition, some advanced training appears desirable in the specific areas of public relations, evaluation of learning and teaching, and research techniques. An internship experience provides the capstone of the formal professional program. This permits the future supervisor to gain on-the-job training and experience under the guidance of an experienced supervisor.

Such a professional education seeks to provide the individual with many of the basic understandings, skills, and processes which may help his work in the schools. It does not pretend to turn out a finished product. The beginning supervisor is simply ready to begin to learn his work. Beyond his basic education, the supervisor's ultimate success is determined by his personality, experiences in the schools, and evolving attitudes and insights in relation to his role.

Skill in teaching. Traditionally, the supervisor is expected to have had several years of successful teaching experience. This judgment is based partly on the logic that if supervisors are to work with and through classroom teachers, they can understand the teacher's role and empathize with him only through personal and direct experience in teaching.

Teaching and supervision both require a high degree of skill in establishing and preserving desirable relationships with others. Thus a person's record of outstanding teaching success attests to such competency. Teaching experience presumably provides for the test-

---

[5] *Educational Supervision—A Leadership Service* (Tallahassee, Fla.: Southern States Work Conference, Florida State Department of Education, 1955), pp. 86–87.

ing of theory in practice, refinement of teaching procedures, deepening of understandings into the basic conditions of learning and teaching, and essential insights into the reactions and characteristics of children and youth.

For the prospective supervisor the opportunity to work with student teachers is highly desirable. The experiences gained from accepting a novice into one's own classroom, helping orient him to the school, seeking to build self-confidence and reasonable security in this first exposure to teaching, supervising the planning and preparation for instruction, evaluating the classroom performance, and guiding his efforts to improve and succeed—all provide a sound introduction to supervision. At the same time, it is likely to sharpen the teacher's awareness of his own strengths and weaknesses.

Variety in teaching experience is also helpful. The elementary supervisor is a stronger resource to the staff if he has taught on several grade levels. The general supervisor in the secondary school is likely to be more successful if he has taught in several subject areas. Supervisors may also profit from teaching in schools of different sizes and locations.

Generally, the faculty is more apt to make use of the services of the supervisor who is known to possess exemplary teaching skill. They react to him as one who has proved himself in the work in which they are engaged and who is likely to be helpful in solving their instructional problems.

Clear perception of roles in the educative process. An important professional attribute is the perspective which the supervisor possesses regarding the overall job of improving instruction. The supervisor should recognize several essential characteristics and relationships in the roles of various persons who cooperatively work for instructional change. For example, the educational leader knows that genuine and long-range changes in classroom procedures result from changes in the thinking, attitudes, and skills of classroom teachers. Thus the impressive number of reports, resource units, course outlines, and lists of recommendations are to little avail unless the teacher himself is induced to change. The supervisor seeks to help the teachers help themselves.

The supervisor must constantly keep in mind that the real focus and desired aims of his work are increased quality and quantity of classroom learning. The school exists simply to provide a setting for the learning-teaching process. The ultimate aim of supervision is to improve this process.

In modern supervision the full-time supervisor acts in a consultative capacity to the teachers and administrative personnel. His is a staff function, which he prefers it to be because it generally results in more productive long-term relationships. He recognizes that the principal of the school is its official administrative head and is directly responsible for the quality of the instructional program. When working in the school building, the supervisor works by permission of the principal and under his general direction. Educational supervision today has become almost by definition the offering of special services and resources without attached administrative authority.

Skill in leadership.   The supervisor needs to possess qualities of leadership. His leadership skills are of two kinds. First, he is a leader himself and second, he fosters leadership in others.

The competent supervisor is ready and able to fulfill leadership responsibilities directly when called upon. He has the facility to see the task clearly and push toward its accomplishment with decisiveness and efficiency. He leads others by his example and by his ability to apply logic and intelligence to the problem. He respects the individuality of others, prizes the potentialities of group members, and delegates responsibility when appropriate.

The supervisor also is skilled in the search for emergent leadership within various groups. He is increasingly able to identify, release, and support leadership potential in whomever the group turns to in a situation. His satisfactions come from the knowledge that a problem has been solved or that a member of the group has made a notable leadership contribution, rather than through recognition and enhanced status for himself.

Knowledge of instructional materials and methods.   A supervisor is generally expected to be familiar with a variety of materials and methods. He must know the advantages and disadvantages of traditional items such as the textbook, workbook, supplementary readings, community resources, and standard audio-visual materials. He should know a great deal about their use and be prepared to work toward improved teaching through these media. He must also keep informed on instructional trends and, especially, emerging developments. He will also be well-acquainted with recent approaches to staff utilization, programmed learning, and educational television. He will know about new approaches and materials resulting from important curriculum study groups.

The supervisor operates as a valuable resource to the teaching staff through his knowledge of the materials and methods of instruction. He presumably has more time and opportunity to attend conventions, to participate in workshops, survey research, and experimentation, and to hear about promising practices in the schools. He may order new materials or descriptions of new procedures, work with teachers to try them out, and report the results to interested educational personnel.

Ability to evaluate and interpret factors in productive learning and teaching. One of the essential skills which the successful supervisor possesses is the ability to visit a classroom teacher in action and discover some of the factors related to the degree of teaching competence observed. Experienced supervisory personnel are able rather quickly to spot symptoms of productive or unproductive teaching.

The learning-teaching process exists within a complex set of human interrelationships among teacher and students. The perceptive supervisor, however, learns to look for key items in making an evaluation. For instance, he senses immediately whether or not the students are in rapport with the teacher. He observes to see if there is a sense of movement and progress in the work or whether it appears aimless and disorganized. He looks for evidences that the learning activity is oriented to clearly understood aims. The observing supervisor seeks to assess the quality of the learning climate. He checks to see if students know fairly well the degree to which they are progressing and whether they are involved at appropriate points in the planning of their work. He is interested in the degree of sensitivity of teachers to student feelings and reactions to classroom experiences. These are examples of learning-teaching characteristics which have special meaning to the alert supervisor.

In addition, the competent supervisor must have the ability to discuss underlying factors with individual teachers and groups. He must work helpfully and constructively to deal with weaknesses. Such effort may involve the positive and practical application of principles of learning and teaching and the clarification of desirable teacher-pupil relationships. He needs to be able to make practical suggestions or point up alternatives which will result in improvement.

Awareness of the importance of process and product. The supervisory worker should develop a professional awareness of the importance of process and product. Both are important in supervision.

The issue of process versus product is most clearly explained by reference to the learning of students in higher education today. Grades have long been regularly and routinely used by teachers to stimulate pupil response and motivate learning. From at least the later elementary school levels through college, the awarding of grades has been used as a means to an end. Today great numbers of college students have completely reversed this relationship. It is apparent that the means has now become the end—students study a subject in order to secure the grade. Their orientation and approach to learning is conditioned by the grade or diploma in view, not by the desire to learn more about the subject, to answer important questions, to satisfy real and personal interests, or to attain mastery of a discipline.

In instructional improvement the supervisor must anticipate probable consequences of both the means used to secure change and the end desired. The end does not always justify the means. For example, undemocratic and dictatorial processes are not justified by the worthy outcomes sought. Before instituting procedures, supervisors should always weigh the probable effects on the staff. In the interests of rapid movement toward a desired change, the supervisor must not be tempted to use great pressure, manipulation, or borrowed administrative authority in a process which quite likely would destroy his usefulness and future productivity as a supervisor. In supervision the product is, of course, of great importance, for the desired change or improvement provides orientation and direction to supervisory efforts. At the same time, however, the process should leave the group of teachers better able to attack and solve subsequent instructional problems, and it ideally should intensify the desirable relationships of the supervisor and the school personnel.

Proficiency in experimentation and research. The person who would become a supervisor needs to develop proficiency in educational experimentation and research. A substantial portion of his work is likely to deal with research. The supervisor regularly reviews the research of others and reports pertinent implications to interested associates. To do this well he must have a background which makes it possible for him to read and analyze such reports.

The supervisor often engages directly in research to assess the quality of the instructional program. He may also work directly or as a consultant with experimentation, both formal and informal, within the school unit. Educational personnel commonly look to the supervisor for specialized assistance in developing a suitable research design, in choosing and applying appropriate statistical treatment to the data, and in summarizing and interpreting the results. Through training, experience, and orientation he must have developed a research point of view. The helpful supervisor will develop a variety of resources which may be placed at the disposal of staff members who are interested in research and experimentation, and he makes himself available to assist in such efforts.

Willingness and ability to continue personal and professional growth. The successful supervisor must continue to grow personally and professionally. It is essential to his long-range happiness, job satisfaction, and maximum competency that he be willing and able to continue such growth.

The beginning supervisor obviously has much to learn. In order to meet the demands of his position, he is impelled to secure new knowledge, explore resources, sample new experiences, and master additional competencies. Similarly, the experienced supervisor necessarily must continue his professional growth. The dedicated supervisor will seek a variety of means to improve his efficiency. He may choose summer courses, workshops, seminars, and conferences in order to further his formal professional education. He will also participate in study groups, informal discussions, cooperative research, and staff meetings with his associates. He should deliberately plan a program of professional reading of new textbooks and of pertinent articles in educational journals, yearbooks, and monographs. Study of nearby instructional experimentation, regular visitation in the schools, and constant contact with students will keep him close to the problems and concerns of the classroom teachers. Membership in professional associations and attendance at national and regional conventions bring the supervisor into contact with highly capable persons who may be equally interested in similar problems. Here he is likely to find people engaged in thinking and working in his own field.

The supervisor must also continue to develop and grow personally. His development as a mature, fully rounded human being must not be neglected. He needs to read widely, engage in productive and satisfying hobby activities, enjoy music and art, satisfy social and recreational interests, and participate fully in family responsibilities. As the supervisor enriches his own personal life and increases his range of interests, he contributes to his supervisory potential.

The foregoing personal and professional qualifications cannot adequately describe the successful supervisor. They can only point to significant and generally pertinent qualities which seem to apply. These items are simply many which officials in colleges and in the public schools find useful when they select candidates for supervisory programs or for actual employment as supervisors.

There is no fixed set of required professional qualities and personal characteristics which guarantees success in supervision. There often may be subtle and intangible aspects of attitude and personality which make the difference between indifferent and outstanding performance. Like all activities which involve the interrelationships of humans, supervision is more nearly an art than a science.

CHAPTER V

Utilizing Group Processes in Supervision

Today many administrators recognize the need for group action in meeting instructional problems. They know that administrative authority and pressure may quickly and efficiently institute "paper changes." The changed behavior is more apparent than real; yet relatively permanent instructional change and improvement will come only as teachers change their attitudes and beliefs. However, because of limited knowledge and lack of experience with genuine democratic group process, such status leaders often are tempted to manipulate groups of teachers so that decisions reached are "safe" —that is, the groups come out with a statement that agrees with what the administrator already has decided. Or the administrators may reserve the really important decisions for themselves and allow groups freedom to deal only with relatively unimportant problems. Supervisors, on the other hand, customarily work in staff positions and are more likely to understand the values and applications of democratic group approaches to curriculum and instruction problems.

The term "group process" as used here refers to the democratic procedures by which a group of individuals identifies, explores, attacks, and attempts to solve a problem of common concern. "The goal of group processes is group productivity, that is, getting something done which could not be done by a single individual." [1] The importance of group process to the supervisor and to the improvement of learning and teaching lies in its ability to broaden the base of involvement and commitment to instructional improvement, to focus the resources of the group on the problem, to increase the ability and satisfaction of individuals in working cooperatively, and to effect significant and lasting changes. A few basic studies [2] have

[1] *Group Processes in Supervision* (Washington, D.C.: Association for Supervision and Curriculum Development, National Education Association, 1948), p. 28.
[2] For a summary of such basic research, see "Twenty-five Years of Educational Research," *Review of Educational Research*, No. 26 (June, 1956), 227–28.

suggested the applications and potential productivity of group process; yet the validation of its worth has generally been demonstrated through its practice in the schools.

Values

Group process offers several highly significant values to educational supervision and staff productivity. When it is handled properly, the following notable effects may be expected.

Staff morale building. Teacher satisfaction and morale are known to be enhanced when teachers regularly and actively participate in educational planning and decision-making.[3] The fact that staff members are involved in democratic interaction which results in decisions thereby increases the understanding of these decisions and their implications. This understanding, in turn, strengthens the loyalty and commitments of the individual members of the group. Such activity is likely to affect the quality of human relationships. Teachers are apt to discover important insights into the personalities of co-workers and to appreciate hidden potentialities and capabilities now revealed. Productive group activity contributes to intercommunication and increases the likelihood that such interrelationships will continue. Group members develop feelings of identity with the staff. Morale and satisfaction with the school in general may be substantially improved.

Individual development of personnel—emergence of leadership. Some of the essential conditions of democratic group process reside in the conscious assumptions that (1) significant contributions may be made by anyone; (2) the basic controls operating in a goal-oriented group come from the common problem to be investigated and from the data pertinent to it; and (3) leadership may be delegated at any time to one or another of the group members. This results ideally in a permissive climate wherein each person does his own thinking, feels free to raise pertinent questions and issues, offers evidence which bears on the question, and exerts leadership when appropriate.

Educational personnel are engaged in joint consideration of a problem of import to all. Individuals are moved to question, exam-

---

3 "Educational Organization, Administration, and Finance," *Review of Educational Research,* No. 25 (October, 1955), 286.

ine, and revise personal beliefs and understandings through such interchange, since there is no official point of view or predetermined solution promulgated by a status leader. Comments or contributions may be judged pertinent or nonpertinent to the issue under discussion; yet the individual members of the group are respected for their views, and full participation is encouraged. In this context, individual teachers are seen to develop personally and professionally, and unsuspected leadership potential is encouraged to emerge.

Shared decision-making—bases better understood. Democratic group problem-solving results in the deepening of understanding of the problem being considered and the bases for the decision reached. When a judgment is made, a decision is reached, and implementing actions are taken by administrative fiat, teachers are likely to comply because of respect for the ability and competence of the principal or because of the realities of administrative authority over them. They are not likely to comprehend fully nor feel strongly the underlying reasons. Group process not only makes it possible to bring a wider variety of resources to bear on the problem, but also it involves the persons who may have to implement the decision in the classroom. Thus the process itself provides teachers with depth of understanding of the problem itself, the reasons for its importance, and the bases for the decision reached.

Implementation of decisions. Given a problem of genuine concern, full participation in its exploration, and shared responsibility for its resolution, the professional staff is likely to follow through with procedures to implement the decision made. The factor of inertia is often said to be the greatest single deterrent to the improvement of learning and teaching. Teachers generally have developed ways of working which seem successful or at least adequate for them, and they naturally resist change. This disinclination to give up established patterns of behavior requires powerful forces to alter. The experience of sharing in decision-making generally is far more effective than inspirational lectures or administrative pressure. As questions are answered and problems resolved, the decision made usually points up desirable implementing activity. To the degree that the participating teacher feels committed to the decision, he also feels impelled to make it work. As a result, he will fully engage in implementing the decision.

Necessary Conditions for
Effective Group Work

Groups work with various degrees of effectiveness. Much of the difficulty in bringing together individuals rests in the need to facilitate the formation of a group rather than simply a collection of individual persons. The conception of group process depends upon the formation of interdependence and cohesiveness among the membership. "When people engage cooperatively in related activity or work toward a common goal, they *create* a group. A group is a plurality of individuals, but what the group does is not plural, but singular." [4]

Actually the working group is something above and beyond the sum total of the individuals involved. The dynamic quality resulting from united efforts and mutual concerns produces a high degree of mutual stimulation, a feeling of identification, and a capacity for increased productivity. The members of a unified group no longer behave as individuals; they submit to some restrictions of freedom and recognize certain obligations to the group in order to gain the benefits of the group process.

Presence of a significant problem. Basic to the operation of group process is the presence of a significant problem which lends itself to group solution. The problem must be real, not simply made up by the principal or supervisor to stimulate some group effort. It must require solution by the staff; it must not be one which may be solved by looking it up in a standard reference text or accessible report.

The problem should be one which is best dealt with by a group. Some questions or difficulties are best handled individually; others require the varied talents and resources of group participants. The problem should lend itself better to discussion in a group context than to solitary reflection. It may need the support of the group to foster acceptance and to implement the solution.

The import of the problem should be felt by the entire group. It needs to be of concern to all if it is to unify the individuals present. Unless every group member feels an identification with the problem and thus is committed to its exploration and solution, the enthusiasm, participation, and group productivity is greatly reduced.

---

4 *Group Processes in Supervision, op. cit.,* p. 24.

Physical atmosphere conducive to problem orientation. Although the advantages of a living room setting are not necessary, certain physical arrangements are desirable. The availability of time is probably first in importance. The group may require substantial amounts of time free from interruptions and competing responsibilities. The situation should be one wherein the group can devote itself to the problem at hand without unnecessary distractions. If individuals customarily drift in and out at various intervals and if persons are called away abruptly and unexpectedly, the continuity and momentum of the group's progress are bound to be impaired. Obviously there are many realities of the school day and pressures of educational responsibilities to be considered. However, the planning of overly brief sessions and scheduling of groups when teachers are fatigued or torn between competing demands should be avoided.

A relatively relaxed social setting is desirable. Comfortable chairs and tables arranged to promote free interchange is more desirable than a classroom setting with rows of chairs facing the teacher's desk. Psychologically the latter is more likely to encourage lectures by the leader than genuine cooperative effort. The serving of refreshments is helpful. In addition, the group may need special facilities, such as a portable chalkboard, a tape recorder, or other pertinent audio-visual resource.

Threat reduction. An essential condition of effective group process is the existence of a climate conducive to free and open exchange of ideas. A democratic and permissive climate frees the individual to think for himself, offer suggestions and comments, and propose solutions without exposing himself to threat of ridicule or rejection by the group. Any group comes to recognize special talents, areas of expertness, and skills among its members. Individuals may differ widely in amount of experience, training, and intelligence; yet each person must be respected as an individual. The contributions of all are prized. Although some may be judged as nonpertinent to the topic under discussion, each is accepted and weighed carefully according to its merits.

Differences of opinion are natural and inevitable. Even though they may prove annoying to group members intent on securing a quick solution, sincere differences expressed by competent and interested personnel strengthen group work and provide one of the most important advantages over solitary cogitation. Staff persons long in the system often are too close to the problem to see some of the important facets. An inexperienced teacher or one new to the system can often approach the problem with more objectivity and perspective. Some individuals habitually play the role of devil's advocate in order to stimulate thinking or state extreme views. The democratic resolution of honest differences leads to growth and superior decision-making. If everyone agrees with everything, real progress is unlikely, or the problem was not real in the first place. Rather than stifling differences in opinion and judgment, the group atmosphere should release and support their expression.

Distributive leadership. In democratic, cooperative group work the leadership is not derived from official status, authority, or position. The concept of group process envisions leadership as residing in the group itself. Every participating member is a potential leader and the group may turn to him at an appropriate point for direction and guidance. Each leader is first of all a member of the group and, second, a temporary leader serving at the pleasure of the group. Group process is a method of shared problem-solving in which all participants are engaged in seeking possible solutions. Anyone in the group who can facilitate progress may be delegated leadership responsibility.

If an outside status official takes charge of the group without its consent, the resulting activity is no longer genuine democratic group process. If a participant usurps leadership using real or implied pressure of administrative authority, the process is distorted or perverted. Of course, individual group members sometimes will attempt to convince others of the soundness of their position; spokesmen of differing positions may negotiate their differences in search of a compromise; and some may speak eloquently and forcefully in attempts to persuade. In democratic group process, however, all remain united by the common goal which they seek, and they submit to the leader who is chosen by the group.

Goal formation. The unity and vitality of the group come from group formulation of the goal. Unless the proposed goal is a result of group decision and claims the allegiance of members, the impetus to group effort will be slight.

A goal imposed upon the group by administrative authority is less likely to motivate the teachers than a goal which they have chosen. Whatever activity that does occur is more due to the pressure of the administrative authority than real concern about the problem. The motivation is extrinsic rather than intrinsic. Participants are not likely to fully comprehend the bases of the problem and the reasons for its importance. Moreover, the goal is apt to appear rigid. There is less chance that it will be subject to modification as the group activity proceeds.

In group process the goal is formulated by the group itself out of common concern. In addition, the goal is held tentatively. The group is flexible in its conception of the goal. As insight is gained into the situation, as the background for the problem is explored, as broader perspective is developed, and as other possibilities become apparent, the goal may be modified.

Consensus. A most crucial period in group work occurs when the decision is about to be made. Well-developed group process seeks to go beyond the customary majority vote used in democratic governmental processes; the goal in group process is consensus.

Reliance on majority rule is rejected in order to retain the unity which has developed in the group. Instead of the majority having to coerce the minority, the majority prefers to try to eliminate the minority by seeking unanimity. In a relatively small group, of course, consensus is a more practicable goal than in a very large one. The similarities among a group of teachers all working within the same school are much more likely to be greater than the differences. Thus the basis for consensus is apt to exist. Moreover, lasting instructional change in the school unit is dependent upon teacher agreement, general support of the change, and unified efforts to put it into practice. Thus the unity in the group is essential to successful implementation of the change.

Search for consensus may be time-consuming and, at times, impossible. If the chances for agreement seem remote at one level, then the group should try to reach consensus at another level. For example, the group may find it impossible to reach unanimous agreement on specific classroom procedures; yet it may find agreement on the general solution to the problem. The task is to establish the points of consensus and leave other areas for subsequent attention by the group. Often consensus is more readily attained if the decision to be made is a tentative one subject to testing and later evaluation. This, of course, is sound problem-solving procedure anyway.

Process awareness. Effective group work depends upon the participants' being aware of the process itself and being willing to submit to the conventions of democratic group activity. Burton and Brueckner assert:

> A group cannot chat itself to truth. The enthusiastic exchange of ignorant opinion is not democratic discussion. The democratic right to participate carries the democratic obligation to stay on the point, to base one's contribution on facts or carefully critical analysis of experience, to accept responsibility.[5]

Participants must possess an abiding faith in the productivity of a group of reasonable individuals who deliberately enter into joint effort to attack a problem of common interest. They must come to prize the worth of logic and the weight of evidence above sheer opinion. They recognize that essential order in the process comes from the goal formulated by the group and the data which are clearly pertinent to it. Direction and progress are marked in relation to the goal, and contributions are judged as to their pertinence to the problem. Ideally, parliamentary procedures are largely irrelevant. If a leader must resort to parliamentary rules of order, the group probably has ceased to function as a unified working body seeking to accomplish a common goal.

Continued evaluation. Evaluation is a continuous part of the desirable group process. As the work of the group moves along, the appraisal seeks evidence in regard to (1) apparent progress toward the goal of the group and (2) the effectiveness of the processes used. The group must make evaluation an integral aspect of the process itself.

Continuing satisfaction depends, at least in part, upon knowledge of movement toward the goal. Cooperative judgments are made by the participants through summaries and progress statements. It is essential that all group members participate in this evaluation and are kept apprised of progress made.

As the group works together democratically, so it also evaluates the process democratically. Process evaluation is carried on so that

---

[5] William H. Burton and Leo J. Brueckner, *Supervision: A Social Process* (New York: Appleton-Century-Crofts, Inc., 1955), p. 184.

ways of working may be improved, participation of the members increased, and more satisfying experiences for all provided. Appraisal such as this is concerned with enhancing the future productivity of group work through refinement of the group procedures and the improvement of individual attitudes and skills in its use.

Limitations of Group Procedures

Group process, of course, is not the answer to all problems of instructional improvement in the schools. It is a specialized, fairly sophisticated technique which is proving to be of great value when used appropriately and well. It does, however, have significant limitations.

Group process is not a procedure for creating ideas. Original, creative ideas do not come simultaneously to all individuals in a group. The process, however, may provide a stimulating setting for the emergence of new ideas. Many persons report that democratic discussion oriented to a conscious goal stimulates them to heightened individual creativity. They may be moved to shake off habitual modes of thinking as different approaches emerge in the group; they may find new points of view or frames of reference; they also may combine familiar facts and information into new ideas and fresh patterns. A major advantage of group work lies in its ability to give participants access to the ideas and insights of others, although it, in itself, should not be expected to produce ideas by which problems are to be solved.

Group work is not equally satisfactory or efficient with groups of different sizes. Simple logistics of handling very large numbers add difficult problems to genuine group process. In larger groups— for example, those with more than thirty persons—it is difficult to promote democratic discussion in which every member finds it easy to participate at appropriate points. Leadership difficulties are compounded and the necessary growth of unity within the group is inhibited.

Not all problems are amenable to group process. Some supervisors become so enamoured with this approach that they encourage its general use even with unsuitable problems and goals. Some questions, for example, may be purely administrative, best left to the line administrator to judge. Others may be too large and comprehensive to be attacked by the group resources available. Some may be too superficial and minute to justify the time spent in group discussion and action. A few problems simply may be insoluble. A great many may best be left to the supervisor working with a few teachers individually.

Effective group process is limited by the inexperience of group members. A professional staff does not ordinarily step into full and productive participation in group work unless they have understanding and practice with the process. Thus groups may be observed operating at various stages of maturity. Some teachers approach group involvement with trepidation because of previous unhappy experiences or attitudes based on hearsay and misunderstanding. Only by practicing the skills and experiencing the satisfactions of productive group effort will these individuals become better participants.

Individuals within the group may inhibit group progress. Occasionally, a teacher or two will seize the opportunity to seek recognition for themselves or for their special area of interest. Sometimes a clash of personalities may disrupt progress and imperil unity. Unintentional pressure developing within the group, as a result of increased momentum and enthusiasm of a majority, may cause certain individuals to block progress or to abandon positions which they hold sincerely and honestly. Group members, of course, possess individual differences in regard to the pace at which they work. Some think slowly and carefully. Others customarily hasten to reach tentative conclusions and then fill in the details. Obviously the pace of the leader or the movement of the group may not fit or satisfy all members. Such limitations do not justify the abandonment of group process. Rather, they suggest some of the realities of its use and identify significant items to be considered before it is instituted.

Phases of Group Procedure

There is no complete blueprint for effective group process for all groups in all situations. Many variables and the democratic process itself make for considerable variation. Group problem-solving, however, generally proceeds through four phases judged to be essential to success.

Identification of a significant problem.   The first phase in group process deals with the identification and acceptance of the problem. Group members are drawn together by the significance of the problem and the degree of concern they feel regarding its solution. Thus the identification and statement of the problem is crucial to the initiation of group work. The group must accept the problem, at least tentatively, in order for genuine group process to begin. Without a problem of common concern there is no purpose or basis for group problem-solving.

Problems may come from many sources inside and outside the school. It may be the result of a comprehensive school-community survey or it may develop through the persistent dissatisfaction of an interested teacher. It might be pointed out by parents, students, or various school personnel. The problem may be recognized through some sort of evaluation, formal or informal, systematic or casual. The important fact is that the group has accepted a problem which it feels is significant and about which it feels it can do something. Such a problem must be clearly stated and carefully defined so that participants generally have a common understanding of its dimensions and importance.

Planning approaches to the solution of the problem.   Once the problem is identified and accepted, the next need is to explore it. The group seeks to bring out pertinent facts, relevant research findings, and applicable principles. Helpful resources of all kinds are sought and brought to bear upon the problem. Often this activity of exploring the problem leads to restatement or redefinition.

Exploration of the problem suggests approaches to the solution. These approaches or lines of attack require careful examination as to practicability and other significant implications. Most important, of course, are judgments in regard to probable success of various proposals. Out of a number of possible approaches, one or more alternative proposals emerge. A generally acceptable solution may be indicated.

Discussion—consensus decision.   Through democratic discussion the group seeks agreement regarding the course of action to be taken. The possible alternative approaches to the solution of the problem are analyzed for probable consequences. Necessary implementing activity is described. Teacher competence to put the change into practice is studied. Only through full discussion of such points may group consensus be reached. The decision which receives group support may be to push vigorously toward instituting the obvious change, to attempt a promising solution, to experiment with several possible improvements, or to make no change at this time. Whatever decision is made must be the product of free and open discussion among group members; it must not be imposed by a status leader. It must represent consensus and thus preserve the unity and mutual support of the group.

Evaluation. As changes are instituted, continuous evaluation provides evidence regarding their worth and establishes bases for revision and replanning. During the group work itself, appraisal procedures indicate progress made and serve to improve subsequent group procedures. Such evaluation is planned and instituted by the group in order to increase its efficiency and promote growth of its members. Some groups delegate evaluative responsibilities to an observer who keeps records as to participation, contributions of resource personnel or consultants, quality of group climate, and leadership behavior. A recorder is customarily chosen to keep track of group progress and direction and to provide progress summaries when needed. Self-evaluation through simple appraisal discussions may periodically be utilized. Individual comments regarding self-growth and satisfactions are solicited. A few groups have used formal rating scales and opinionnaires to secure information. Even a routine check of attendance may be revealing.

The supervisor's role in the process. The supervisor must perform a difficult role in group process. First of all he is, and must remain, a participating member of the group. At times he may grow impatient with others less experienced in group procedures, but he cannot usurp leadership without destroying, or at least impairing, the process. He will, of course, accept the leadership role when the group desires it. He must, however, recognize the need to identify and utilize the leadership potential residing in other group members.

Because of his superior knowledge and experience in group process, he may act as a resource to the group in its planning, organization, and evaluation. He may also provide information, data, reports of experimentation, and other such resource materials upon request. As a member of the group his intelligence, training, and experience are committed to attainment of the group goal.

The supervisor works to secure optimum conditions for successful group experience. He tries within the group to promote the necessary climate of cooperation, democracy, and mutual support. He may seek to persuade administrative leaders to provide the time, freedom from interruptions, and the essential physical facilities for productive group effort. Most of all he demonstrates by personal example his respect for the worth of other participants and his confidence in the ultimate success of group process.

CHAPTER VI

Types of Group Procedures
Utilized by Supervisors

Teachers and other educational personnel have been involved in group procedures for many years. Some of these groups have been set up primarily for administrative purposes. School principals have used faculty and staff meetings to disseminate information to the professional staff, to explain and interpret school board policies, to secure the cooperation of the faculty in regard to school regulations, to have required forms filled out and signed, and to obtain information from their teachers. As the theory of group process developed and application to groups in the schools demonstrated its worth, the supervisor came to utilize a wide variety of procedures for the purposes of guiding teacher growth and assisting in the improvement of instruction.

Supervisory persons have utilized a wide variety of group meetings for possible contributions. They generally have come to feel that many different kinds of group procedures are needed to provide varied settings in which teacher growth may occur. They have developed new patterns of group work which seem appropriate to many different problems and to school units of various sizes. They have endeavored to strengthen traditional group organizations and have encouraged teachers to take advantage of the meetings and conferences sponsored by professional associations.

The competent supervisor must utilize a variety of groups in his task of improving the learning-teaching process. If one recognizes that supervision is concerned with any activity which contributes to the self-confidence, security, continuing improvement, and growth of teachers, then many different group procedures may be valuable to this end.

Orientation Meetings for New Teachers

A crucial task of some urgency is the need to orient new teachers to the school unit in which they will work. Many school systems, especially the larger ones, plan preschool orientation meetings for new teachers. The most successful of these have been planned around the most obvious needs of the new faculty members. Some of the teachers are just beginning to teach; all are new to the particular school system. The orientation program should provide important assistance to all of them.

The new teachers require orientation to the community which is served by the school and in which they probably will live. Thus the meeting should provide information about socio-economic levels, ethnic groups, occupational patterns, geographical features, and historical development. Sometimes bus tours are provided to help teachers see the homes and neighborhoods from which their students come and to provide an overall view of the community itself. Recreational and cultural resources of the area are pointed out.

The meeting should orient teachers to the school. Essential materials or teacher handbooks are distributed and explained. These commonly cover such items as school system policies and regulations, school philosophy, record systems, services available, program of studies, and school routine (for example, length of school day, length of class periods, regular and assembly schedules). Administrative and supervisory personnel are introduced, and relationships and ways of working are explained. The new teachers are taken on a tour of the school plant and are shown their assigned rooms. They receive their individual teaching assignments if they do not have them already. Resources and materials for instruction are pointed out. Plans and probable school developments in the near future are discussed.

New teachers need help in resolving personal problems. They often need assistance in finding satisfactory housing. They usually desire information and explanation regarding sick leave, tenure procedures, retirement, salary schedule or merit pay provisions, health insurance, and credit union. Many of them appreciate knowing about churches, art centers, museums, musical groups, municipal libraries, drama organizations, and other cultural advantages. Leisure time and recreational facilities should be described.

The school district may choose an orientation committee consisting of administrators, supervisors, and teachers. This committee often includes some second and third year teachers who, having recently gone through this experience, obviously would have some ideas regarding needs and concerns of new teachers.

Orientation meetings for new teachers commonly provide time and opportunity for questions from the new faculty. This meeting assures that many of the pressing concerns which have not been adequately covered are identified and handled. These meetings tend to range from two days to a week in length in large systems and from one to two days in small systems. Obviously there are many advantages to such a meeting when it is planned to deal with the pressing needs of new teachers; yet a common complaint indicates that often too much information is given. The new teachers meet so many new people, undergo so many new experiences, and gather so much information that some are confused and all tend to forget much of what they learned unless subsequent help is given. The general conclusion is that orientation meetings for new teachers are valuable supervisory procedures, although the teachers may require additional orientation assistance during the school year.

Preterm Planning Meetings for All Teachers

A practice which is solidly established in a number of schools is the preterm planning meeting. Although specific arrangements and organization vary from place to place, the general purposes tend to be quite similar. The preschool meeting for all teachers is a procedure which brings together the entire staff in order to give attention to problems of broad interest and concern to the school. Widespread participation and involvement of the faculty are sought. The location in time of this meeting is especially desirable because teachers are full of anticipation for the coming school year and the pressure of daily teaching responsibilities has not yet begun. This pressure often prevents full attention and participation in subsequent meetings.

Although such meetings are held many times at the school building, some schools prefer to arrange them in locations which promote a high degree of informality and a minimum of customary status relationships. The staff may meet at a nearby park, lake, or campground facility. Occasionally, the families of school personnel may be invited and social and recreational activities organized.

The planning is carefully done by the supervisor and teachers. The choice of problems and areas to be explored is vital to the success of the meeting. If involvement and participation is to be worthwhile, teachers must feel that these topics are important to the school and themselves or that they have had a part in their formulation. Often college and university persons will give of their special expertness, recognize the primacy of teacher problems and areas, and resist the temptation to lecture at the participants.

Large Group Conferences

The supervisor makes use of various kinds of large group conferences in guiding teacher growth and directly attacking a variety of problems. Some of these are valuable to individual teachers by stimulating thinking, broadening perspective, developing a feeling of identification with a professional group, acquainting them with new developments in teaching, and the like. Others are organized to deal with problems of mutual concern within the school unit.

Conventions. Increasing attention is being given to the values of teacher attendance and participation at conventions of different kinds. At the national level the most popular and, as judged by teachers, the most valuable are those held by subject or special interest organizations (for example, the National Council of Teachers of English, the National Council for the Social Studies, the National Science Teachers Association, the International Reading Association). Many of these offer general programs of broad interest as well as specific section meetings oriented to special problems of both elementary and secondary school teachers. Here the interested faculty member is likely to find others who have similar concerns and who are thinking, planning, trying, and doing something about their problems.

Membership is growing rapidly in such organizations, and attendance at national conventions is increasing because more teachers are being urged to participate. Supervisors encourage teachers to attend. Some school systems each year provide even more tangible encouragement by offering payment of partial or even full expenses to a few interested teachers and by providing substitute teachers to free them from teaching responsibilities. Satisfaction is often enhanced through the opportunity to report their experiences to colleagues and to introduce the new ideas into their own schools.

State conventions are typically held annually and, of course, have the advantage of being closer at hand. In states which have large geographical areas and widely scattered population centers, the state teachers' association may divide the convention into several divisions, all of which meet at the same time and are spaced geographically so that every teacher may find a meeting which is reasonably accessible to him. The schools are usually closed during the state convention, thus freeing teachers to sample the great variety of meetings offered. Administrators and supervisors encourage teachers to attend the general meetings, which are intended to provide inspiration, to inform, and to clarify important issues of broad interest. They also stress attending the meetings and luncheons which bring together educational personnel with similar school assignments and concerns. These section meetings are organized by teachers and supervisors who make up subject-matter or special interest sections within the state teachers' association. These meetings sometimes are planned less skillfully than those at the national level, but they are usually more directly oriented to the problems and educational conditions of the state. Moreover, the supervisor can correctly point out to the faculty that the sessions are conceived and arranged by fellow teachers within the state and not by some remote group which presumably has little knowledge of local needs and no association with state programs.

Local conferences commonly involve persons from several school systems but are not large enough to be classed as a state convention. These may be sponsored by various educational groups or by local organizations. For example, a metropolitan area English association might arrange a meeting to discuss various problems of common interest to English teachers in the urban and suburban schools in that locality. Educational leaders from several adjacent school districts might pool resources and ideas in order to arrange a large group conference of great import to their teachers. A small group of local teachers' associations might join forces to sponsor a meeting for the benefit of their members. Here the planning is even more real to local educational personnel. The meetings can be tailored to fit the interests of the area teachers and their particular problems. Thus teacher involvement and participation are likely to be increased.

The supervisor consciously attempts to utilize the great number of available conferences and conventions in his work of improving instruction. Within the profession many groups at the national, state, and local levels offer programs which may provide significant experiences to teachers who attend. The supervisor sometimes contributes to the important planning of some of these; he continually seeks to encourage teachers to attend and participate; and he works to convince administrators to make provisions which enable them to take advantage of such meetings.

Teachers' meetings. The faculty meeting is a frequently used and sometimes abused group procedure in the schools. Its use as an administrative device is well-established. The whole faculty meeting brings together all teachers and other educational workers within a school unit so that some administrative matters may be expeditiously handled. For example, announcements may be made to all teachers; forms may be distributed, filled out, and collected on the spot; the administrator's time is saved by speaking to the whole staff in a single group rather than in a number of smaller groups; information may be disseminated and interpreted to everyone in the same way. Teachers' reactions to faculty meetings, however, often have been negatively influenced through faulty administrator practices. The principal or superintendent who regularly distributes mimeographed copies of the school announcements or a description of a new policy and then proceeds to read this same material at great length, or the administrator who regularly chooses to lecture his captive audience about their shortcomings with the mistaken notion that this will inspire them, will invariably contribute to distaste for staff meetings. However, teachers' meetings can become an important supervisory procedure.

Through the cooperation of administrative, supervisory, and instructional personnel working on a planning committee, the staff meeting can be set up to deal with topics or problems which teachers recognize as being important to them and the school. The staff is notified in advance regarding the agenda to be discussed and thus have time to think about it beforehand. The meetings are scheduled so that teachers can plan to attend. Time and location of the meetings are conducive to relaxed, relatively uninterrupted activity. The length of the sessions is varied according to the nature of the discussion planned; the meetings are varied in format and in the processes used.

Teachers' meetings which bring together the entire faculty should deal with curriculum and instructional matters of broad and general import to the total program, while more specific matters involving a particular subject area or a single elementary grade should be handled in departmental or grade level meetings. For example, overall grading practices, promotion policies, proposed adoption of a multiple diploma system, and general articulation problems of students moving from elementary school to junior high school are broad topics often suitable for whole faculty meetings. Principals customarily chair the staff meetings held for administrative purposes, but they often find it desirable to allow a supervisor or teacher to lead the discussion when the topic is a problem which deals directly with the improvement of curriculum or instruction. The administrator does not necessarily withdraw from the group. He should remain, in the best democratic sense, a member of the group, for he may be an important resource in exploring and attempting to solve the problem. He should contribute when appropriate, but he should not dominate the discussion from the sidelines. The supervisor recognizes the potential of general faculty meetings, for productive group work is possible any time common interests cause discussion among a large portion of the faculty.

High schools customarily are organized by academic departments, and much important work can be handled in the departmental faculty meeting. Obviously the department is concerned with problems related to the subject area which is common to all its staff members. Departmental meetings customarily focus on such matters as selection of new textbooks, sequential placement of subject-matter topics, vertical articulation among different courses, relationships of elective and required courses within the subject area, formulation of departmental objectives, and improvement of evaluative procedures. Given a department chairman or head who is chosen for his outstanding ability as a teacher and his qualities of leadership, and given the assistance of a competent supervisor, the departmental faculty meeting can become highly satisfying and helpful to the teachers involved. Beginning teachers especially prize the opportunity to work closely with older, more experienced teachers in dealing with specific instructional problems close to them all.

One important limitation of the departmental meeting is that it tends to compartmentalize the faculty and the curriculum. Each department concerns itself with its own portion of the curriculum and, unless other procedures are instituted, the learner is likely to become secondary to subject matter. For this reason grade level meetings are organized by the supervisor. Here teachers of various subjects meet to consider the program of a particular grade level. The total experience of the learner tends to be the focus of attention. Integration, correlation, horizontal articulation among subjects, and consistency of instruction, evaluation, and grading procedures are examples of important considerations of such meetings.

Elementary schools commonly find it less difficult to retain perspective of the child and his total experience in school than high schools do. Because so many elementary teachers work in schools organized by self-contained classrooms, they teach the same group of children for the major part of the day and are constantly dealing with the problem of balance and coordination among the many subjects to be taught. Elementary schools tend to be smaller in size and whole faculty meetings are common. However, teachers' meetings of a single grade level, or of the primary grades or upper grades, are often held to discuss appropriate problems. Meetings which deal with such problems as reading, arithmetic, handwriting, or spelling may be productive group procedures also.

Teachers' meetings as a supervisory device are important to the growth of teachers and the improvement of learning and teaching. When well-handled and carefully planned, they may help satisfy the social needs of teachers, develop feelings of belonging and identification with the staff, and resolve differences among subgroups and individuals, as well as lead to the identification, analysis, and solution of significant instructional problems.

Small Group Conferences

Within a large faculty not all the teachers are equally concerned with a particular problem or difficulty. The staff is composed of a group of persons possessing varied backgrounds of experience, training, strengths, weaknesses, and ambitions. One of the great and abiding satisfactions of teachers who are alert to new developments, experimentally inclined, and anxious to improve, is the fact that they can usually find a few like-minded colleagues. Such clusters of individuals are drawn to each other and offer mutual support and encouragement. Supervisors are coming to recognize the value of small group procedures as one way of working toward upgrading instruction. They encourage the development of study groups and seminars within the staff.

Study groups. Study groups commonly begin informally, often accidentally, as a few teachers find themselves seeking each other's company in order to discuss a topic of mutual interest or concern. The group simply begins to meet more or less regularly to share ideas. Although loosely organized, the group is held together and sustained in its efforts by the problem and the mutual stimulation of the shared interest. Meeting times may be determined by a common planning period, arrangements to lunch together, or agreement to get together one evening a week at a member's home. The discussion is based on a real and burning interest in a common problem growing out of the particular responsibilities of the participants. The supervisor may be drawn into the group as a resource or may provide assistance at appropriate points when requested. When the problem is resolved or the interest satisfied, the study group is likely to dissolve as quietly and informally as it was born.

Seminars. The seminar represents a somewhat more formalized organization than the study group. If a small number of teachers come to recognize the need for a more formal arrangement, a more systematic approach to the problem, or an awareness that they do not possess among themselves the knowledge and resources to significantly attack the problem, they are likely to utilize the supervisor's assistance in setting up a seminar. As a more formal procedure the seminar group tends to schedule regular meetings and chooses someone to coordinate the activity.

The coordinator or seminar leader may be a supervisor, one of the group members, or an outside person. His main task is to help the group systematically accomplish what it sets out to accomplish. Commonly a resource person or consultant is invited to work with the seminar group often on a long-term basis. He may be a central office supervisor, an experienced person from a neighboring school district, a consultant from the state department of education or the office of the county superintendent of schools, or a university or college professor. His function is to bring a real measure of expertness to the seminar group. Through study, research, or experience he is qualified to assist a group of interested people to learn more about a certain area of concern. He performs this role best not by lecturing, but by facilitating group consideration of the problem. Naturally he offers his expertness and resources when pertinent, but he must not inhibit the group as it engages in sustained, free discussion.

Many school districts make provisions by which outside coordinators or consultants are paid for their services and, in this way, expert assistance may be secured. The unifying problem area to be dealt with is vital to success and continuing interest and participation. However, because the seminar is a sustained, long-term activity, the group members commit themselves in advance to stay with it during the scheduled period.

Small group procedures pose difficulties of scheduling and arranging. They sometimes appear inefficient, for many different small groups may be working on different things at the same time. The supervisor, however, recognizes that the topics under discussion are likely to be real and close to the teachers. The focus of the activity is specifically on problems which come out of current instructional responsibilities. Moreover, participation is likely to be full and involvement deeply felt. Such conditions foster deep and lasting changes in the faculty involved, far more so than most large group procedures which deal with more general and abstract topics.

Teacher Committee Work

Today administrators and supervisors make considerable use of teacher committee procedures. Many committees at both the school district level and the individual school level are employed. This increasing emphasis is the result of more democratic school administration concepts, knowledge of the productive potential of teacher committee work, and recognition of the positive effects of teacher participation on staff morale.

Some committees are temporary, set up to deal with a specific problem and released when it is resolved; others are relatively permanent, organized to provide for sustained, long-term work on a major problem in the schools. The committee membership may be appointed by administrator and supervisor or elected by the staff. Some committees are set up as representative groups to advise the administration on school matters, to facilitate communication among the staff members, particularly at different levels, and to contribute to planning which affects the whole staff. Other committees are chosen primarily as action groups to engage in group problem-solving for the benefit of the school unit.

At the school district level vertical committees are commonly found. These committees, composed of teachers representing all the grades from kindergarten through the twelfth grade, study a problem or curriculum area which runs throughout the school system. Large school systems institute horizontal committees that include educational personnel from various schools within the district. For example, there may be a committee in which selected teachers representing all the junior high schools participate. Similar unit committees may be organized for the primary grades, intermediate grades, and senior high schools in the school system.

Area committees may also be valuable supervisory devices. A common pattern for this committee involves teachers from a central high school and all the elementary schools within the system. This committee may be especially suitable for studying the community which the schools serve and for exploring and attacking such problems as articulation between school levels and continuity of learning.

Special committees, planned and organized to deal with a special problem, are found at both district and individual school levels. Committee members are chosen because they possess special competences and interest in the area of concern. A system-wide special committee might be charged with securing information and teacher opinion, exploring various possibilities, and making a specific proposal regarding such issues as provisions for merit pay, handling controversial issues in the classroom, and teacher leave for advanced study or travel. Individual schools customarily have existing departmental and/or grade level organization which provides for teacher meetings to discuss various topics. The special committee, however, may also be utilized to bring together a smaller, specially interested group of educational personnel to work more systematically and directly on a specific problem. Examples of topics on which such building committees might work include homework, eligibility requirements for extraclass participation, needed audio-visual facilities in the building, report cards, criteria for the charter of high school clubs, and additional play equipment desired.

The products and values of teacher committee work are varied. Concrete proposals, status descriptions, recommended policy statements, curriculum guides, resource units, suggested practices, increased teacher understanding, faculty growth, and improved morale are examples of the important outcomes which may accrue. Most supervisors are aware of the occasional teacher complaint that after much committee time, labor, and sincere deliberation, the recommendations of the committee were ignored. This points up the need to charge the committee, particularly the special committee, with explicit tasks or problems and to make certain that areas of responsibility and the nature of the contribution expected of the committee are clearly understood. A major problem lies in the difficulty of securing released time for committee members so that they may devote a full measure of effort and attention to significant committee problems.

Teachers' Councils

Some teachers customarily participate as members of various school councils. Although there is some overlap in conception of the council and certain kinds of teacher committees, the council tends to be a group which emphasizes advisory, planning, and policy-making functions. The factor of representation is likely to be vital in such a group. If the administrator seeks to use a council of teachers as a sounding board or relies heavily on its advice, he assumes that the views of the total faculty are represented. When planning is accomplished that affects all teachers, the individual staff member should feel that he is genuinely represented on the council. Policy decisions likewise demand adequate representation. Usually the council is rather formal in its organization and operation. Meetings are regularly scheduled and agenda items carefully planned. Once established the council generally is considered a permanent group, although provisions for rotating membership are made.

Different types of councils are utilized for various purposes. For example, a cooperative council, consisting of representatives from all elementary schools in the system, may consider appropriate problems and advise the administrators and faculty members. A coordinating council may plan and organize the formal in-service activities of the school district. An advisory council of teachers may be formed to work with the superintendent; it operates parallel to the administrative council, which is made up of school district administrators. A community-school council may bring together school personnel and lay citizens to discuss such topics as public relations, the relationship of school and other educative agencies to the community, evaluation of the prevocational and vocational preparation of students, community use of school buildings and facilities, safety programs, and opportunities for adult education.

Action and Experimental Research

All supervisors are necessarily concerned with research. One of their important tasks is to read and communicate to others the educational research which is pertinent to their school situations. They are consumers and interpreters of this research. In addition, they often may carry out research themselves at the direction of the administration or to discover points to apply supervisory effort. They are, however, in a position to make important contributions through group research.

Whenever a group of teachers becomes interested in systematically attacking a problem area, the possibility of some degree of research activity is present. The experienced supervisor recognizes the benefits of research to the teachers involved and to the school unit itself. He also knows that he is likely to be called upon to supply vital research skills and assistance.

Occasionally, research of considerable precision and careful design, deserving of the term "experimental research," may occur. In today's schools, however, the research activity is more often action research. Action or cooperative research, a fairly recent development of group work by teachers in local schools, may be a valuable supervisory procedure, for it typically (1) is carried out by the faculty members themselves with the possible assistance of a research consultant, (2) involves problems which are perceived to be important in the particular situation at hand, (3) is aimed at producing improvement or change in the local setting, although it may incidentally have broader significance, and (4) combines the research activity with in-service growth of teachers as its goals.

Such research directly engages the teachers and their students in their regular work. Ordinarily many alert teachers try new techniques and instructional materials; yet this is often done informally, almost haphazardly, and the new procedure is retained or rejected on the basis of hunch and intuition. Action research seeks to provide order precision to such a process. It is the systematic identification and analysis of a problem, organized attempts at amelioration, and the careful evaluation of these changes carried out in the school setting, rather than under carefully controlled laboratory conditions. It prizes objectivity, logic, and the weight of evidence in the process.

The supervisory person must work carefully with groups of teachers who are relatively untrained in research techniques. Often the exceptionally fine teacher who is flexible, extremely sensitive to the reactions and feelings of learners, individualistic, and somewhat jealous of his freedom may not welcome the restrictions which co-operative research sometimes brings until he comes to understand something of the nature and conditions of research. Part of the job of the supervisor, participating with groups of interested teachers, is to help them develop research skills and a research point of view.

One of the most crucial steps in action research, which requires special assistance from the supervisor or research consultant, is problem identification.[1] This activity begins with each teacher's statement of his particular concern. From a number of these statements the group, with help from the consultant, seeks the underlying problem. With untrained persons it may take some care to identify and state a problem which is realistic and practicable in terms of the resources, abilities, time available, and energy limitations of the teachers involved. The research problem must be specific but not too narrowly conceived or preoccupied with details. It should not be stated so as to depend on questionable assumptions or to imply obvious solutions. Other stages in the research—formulating a hypothesis, testing the promising solution, evaluating the change

---

[1] See Hilda Taba, "Problem Identification," in *Research for Curriculum Improvement* (Washington, D.C.: Association for Supervision and Curriculum Development, National Education Association, 1957).

according to the evidence gathered and compared to the old procedures, and continuous subsequent appraisal of the results—demand systematic, orderly effort if sound outcomes are to be achieved.

The supervising person needs to promote essential conditions which facilitate research in the school. For example, support and encouragement by the administrator are necessary. Because of his central status role the principal can motivate or effectively block research efforts. Actually, the principal often feels strong pressures toward productivity. He is rewarded when his staff is observed trying new techniques and solving problems. At the same time, however, he feels even greater pressure to be "safe"; that is, he does not want the research to stir parents to criticism or to develop jealousies among his staff. For this reason he may not accord the research group the right to fail. Supervisors, of course, know that it is unrealistic to expect every attempt at improvement to be an unqualified success, no matter how painstakingly considered and judiciously implemented. Every research attempt carries with it the risk of failure. It is essential that groups willing to experiment intelligently and carefully be given this right.

As with all types of group procedures utilized by supervisors, cooperative research is likely to benefit the participants themselves as well as directly influence instructional practices. The effective supervisor must know the possibilities inherent in various group procedures and seek to employ them to best advantage in his work.

CHAPTER VII

The Supervisor Works with Individual Teachers

Even though group procedures have increasingly been used with good results in supervision, the supervisor tends to feel that some of his most effective and satisfying work is accomplished with individual teachers. Procedures in which the supervisor offers assistance and attention to individual teachers are time-consuming and demand great portions of a supervisor's work-load; yet such a relationship possesses several very important potential advantages. Teachers' individual differences are best discovered and dealt with most constructively in the individual teacher-supervisor relationship. The supervisor and teacher are often able to establish close and relatively stable bases for cooperative work. The supervisor is able to secure specific and concrete information about the teacher, the students assigned to the teacher, and the particular classroom situation. The teacher is likely to secure assistance and counsel regarding his own unique problems and needs. He often will develop enough confidence in the supervisor to reveal concerns and deficiencies which never would be brought out in a group context. Certainly the individual teacher-supervisor procedure has a vital part to play in the total supervisory effort.

Classroom Visitation

Classroom visitation or observation is an old supervisory technique. Today it must be carefully handled because of its popular use as an administrative device for inspecting and rating teachers. Teachers, of course, must be evaluated for retention, dismissal, or tenure purposes; classroom visitation provides the rater with a sample of instructional performance. This is not the whole picture, to be sure; yet it is a convenient method which allows the busy administrator to come to some sort of conclusion. The supervisor, on the other hand, if released from the task of rating teachers, looks at classroom visitation from a different viewpoint.

Through today's conception of supervision as a process marked by cooperation and democratic principles, the activity of observation takes on a constructive orientation. The supervisor attempts to dispel any uneasiness and fear by focusing his attention on the teaching situation itself. He works to promote the understanding of his staff role; he seeks to work as a peer, interested in helping the teacher improve the learning-teaching situation of which the teacher is but one aspect. He does nothing to threaten the teacher's status, for this is certain to cause rigidity and defensiveness and will inhibit improvement. Ideally conceived and executed, the observation is initiated by teacher request and is aimed at a problem which teacher and supervisor have agreed to attack cooperatively. In practice, however, some school systems suffer from inadequate programs of supervision marked by over-dependence upon infrequent, poorly planned, inspectional visitation.

Purposes. Visitation for administrative purposes has little relevance to supervision. Wiles asserts, "Observation as a phase of rating is a procedure that restricts the improvement of teaching." [1] If, however, the classroom observation is more directly concerned with the learning of the students than the performance of the teacher, more beneficial results are likely. Moreover, the state of knowledge of methodology does not reveal a precise, clearly correct model for teaching. There is no carefully defined set of classroom activities which has been demonstrated to work equally well for all. Effective and creative teachers are observed working in different ways according to personality differences, variation in educational goals and purposes, and different student groups. Therefore, the supervisor must analyze the teacher's performance mainly as it influences the learning of students.

The overall purpose of observation is to study the learning-teaching process. More specifically, the purposes of classroom visitation have been stated by Boardman, Douglass, and Bent as the study of:

1. The materials the pupils are to learn, their validity for the objectives of education, their utility, interest, and value for the pupils, and their adaptation to the pupils' abilities and needs.

---

[1] Kimball Wiles, *Supervision for Better Schools* (Englewood Cliffs, N.J.: Prentice-Hall, Inc., 1950), p. 259.

2. The means used to stimulate and guide pupils' learning, the psychological principles used and their application to the specific learning to be acquired.

3. The means used in discovering, diagnosing, and remedying the learning difficulties of pupils.

4. The means used for evaluating the learning product, the nature and means of the methods of measurement, and their relation to the goals of the learning situation.[2]

The supervisor may not attempt to assess all aspects of the classroom situation at once; this requires great experience and skill even to attempt. He is more apt to focus his attention on an area of difficulty which he and the teacher jointly have agreed needs improvement. Even when asked to observe generally, he tends to look for items which he has found to be crucial in productive learning and teaching, or at least symptomatic of basic problems. He might check something as specific and obvious as the amount of time taken by pupils in distributing and returning materials. He is likely to attend to evidences that students see purpose and direction in their work. He may note whether students are generally cooperative in their work or whether they are highly competitive. The quality of classroom climate, the degree of teacher sensitivity to student feelings and reactions, the nature of pupil-teacher interactions, the opportunity for students to evaluate their own work, and the freedom from rigidity and opportunity for creativity are other possible important areas for the supervisor's attention.

In observing for supervisory reasons, the purpose for the visit should be clearly understood by both supervisor and teacher. High productivity and minimal teacher anxiety are more likely to result if the visit is judged to be essential to exploring and resolving a problem which is recognized by the teacher. The visitation is simply one phase in the cooperative attempt to improve instruction.

Types of visitation. Classroom visitation is generally of three types: (1) announced, (2) unannounced, and (3) by invitation. Where the visitation is for the purpose of rating or some other administrative reason, the type of visitation takes on special significance. However, the concept of classroom observation by the supervisor as a means of data gathering for use in cooperative

---

[2] C. W. Boardman, H. R. Douglass and R. K. Bent, *Democratic Supervision in Secondary Schools* (Boston: Houghton Mifflin Company, 1953), p. 144.

problem-solving largely resolves this controversy. There is no need for the teacher to put on a special show to impress the visitor. By the same token the visitor does not have to try to catch the teacher in a more or less typical teaching performance. Instead, the teacher and supervisor plan what class or what classroom activity is to be observed. Thus in a real sense the supervisor increasingly visits by invitation. He may be invited to observe a particular lesson on a particular day. He may seek data on the results of a new teaching procedure and schedule a series of visits with several individual teachers, or he may simply feel free to drop in unannounced. Without the need to rate or inspect and with the establishment of rapport, the visitation is likely to be at the request of the teacher or by mutual agreement.

With beginning teachers and teachers new to the system, the type of visitation may need special consideration. The announced or scheduled observation allows teachers to specially prepare the students and the lesson. It could, however, make some inexperienced teachers highly nervous and apprehensive, so that their work would not be typical of their normal teaching. Most supervisors have rather heavy work loads and they may need to schedule their visitation time carefully. In this case the announced visitation usually guards against visiting during the administration of a test, the showing of a motion picture, a period devoted to free reading, or a class working in the library.

The unannounced visitation has the advantage of sampling the regular work of teacher and students. It frees the supervisor to schedule his time to his own best advantage, even though he occasionally may find classroom activity which leaves little for him to see. Of course, some teachers may be nervous at his unexpected appearance. Moreover, the supervisor may have some sort of reason or purpose for the visit, but the teacher may not. Thus the potential productivity of the observation is reduced.

Length and frequency of visits. In supervision the length and frequency of visits are determined by the purpose of the visitation. For example, if the inexperienced teacher recognizes some difficulty but is not sure of the causes or contributing factors, the supervisor may need to observe for several times until the problem is identified. If the teacher is trying out a new method or introducing a new instructional material, the visit may be scheduled specifically in order to observe this activity.

Generally it is desirable to see the teaching as a whole. In secondary schools the supervisor will probably seek to observe the entire class period. In the elementary schools the visitor will attempt to observe the whole spelling lesson, reading activity for the day, or arithmetic drill. He tries to see a unified activity or planned lesson from initiation to conclusion. Often the teaching procedures used are crucial to the productivity of the learning-teaching process— for example, stimulating interest, providing pertinent backgrounds of experience or recalling relevant past experience, planning the proposed activity with students, or making important assignments. Similarly, the concluding activities by which learning is reinforced —that is, important points summarized, student satisfaction enhanced, and bridges made to a subsequent lesson—are especially vital. Moreover, the supervisor usually needs to prepare for the visit by studying the teacher's planning and the materials of instruction in order to know where the teacher is in his work and to understand what his goals and purposes are. In this way the observer is better able to interpret what he sees in the classroom.

The inexperienced teacher and the teacher new to the school may need more frequent visitation than the experienced teacher long in the school system. The latter is aware of the policies and ways of working and presumably is in agreement with the philosophy of the school. He knows the community and the student group with whom he works. In addition, he and the supervisor are well-acquainted and are likely to have established satisfying cooperative relationships. The new teacher, on the other hand, needs helpful orientation to the school, may require early assistance and encouragement as he meets new and different problems, and must come to understand the services and resources of the supervisor which are available for his benefit. In addition, teachers who have severe problems or who are engaged in instructional experimentation or action research undoubtedly will require frequent observation.

Follow-up devices. There should be a follow-up of every classroom visitation. The supervisor and teacher must cooperatively examine the results of the observation. This is best accomplished through a post-visitation conference. Depending on the purpose of the observation, the supervisor will prepare some kind of record or report to be used as a basis for the follow-up discussion. In the past many different checklists, evaluative records, observation guides, and report sheets have been proposed. These, however, were planned for the purpose of inspecting or rating the teacher and have limited utility for supervisory personnel today.

The purpose of the visitation will determine the nature of the written supervisory report—for example, if the supervisor and teacher are cooperatively engaged in evaluating a new instructional practice, seeking the cause of student apathy, securing data regarding present procedures, checking responses of a particular pupil, or assessing the quality of the learning-teaching climate. Often the most helpful record of the visit takes the form of a simple diary of the classroom activity. The factual description without evaluative comments is used as a basis for cooperative analysis. Teacher and supervisor examine the record, formulated by the supervisor who is not absorbed in the direct teaching and who observes the activity from a different perspective in the room. It is desirable not to mix the observer's evaluations or opinions in the description, for the teacher must have the opportunity to discuss what happened and why, without having his judgment distorted by someone else's evaluations. The discussion will center on the classroom activity as interpreted and appraised through two different points of view. In any event the teacher should receive a copy of the written record. Other devices are sometimes used, such as tape recordings, discussion flow or participation charts, and time analyses of various activities. All such supervisory procedures must contribute to cooperative analysis of the problem and to constructive measures for subsequent improvement.

Teachers recognize that visitation is an integral part of the supervisory program. They generally expect to be observed. They prefer, however, to have a voice in regard to the purpose and nature of the visits. They generally realize the potential values of cooperative problem attack and the contributions that observation by an objective, well-trained supervisor can make to their professional productivity.

Individual Conferences with Teachers

Individual conferences with teachers provide one of the most productive settings for supervisory work. In many such conferences the supervisor and teacher meet as equals, both interested in solving an instructional problem. Some conferences, especially with inexperienced teachers, may be more in the nature of a counseling session. Often the conference is simply a device for securing information or working out details. Sometimes it is aimed at resolving differences and establishing relationships. The conference has the great advantage of providing for a direct and intimate interaction between supervisor and teacher, both of whom are interested in improving instruction.

Purposes and types. The supervisor utilizes individual conferences for different purposes. Obviously the classroom visitation requires accompanying conference activity. Every observation should be followed by an individual conference if it is to be productive and minimally threatening to the teacher. Quite often the visitation will be preceded by a conference at which the purpose of the visit or the problem to be attacked is cooperatively arranged. Thus one type of conference is an essential part of the visitation procedure.

Unplanned conferences may be valuable to the supervisor in establishing rapport and gaining insight into the teacher's attitudes toward teaching, satisfaction in his job, and individual ambitions and aspirations. These informal talks, often quite brief, may open up problems and concerns which become the bases for later supervisory work. The alert supervisor is always ready to make use of such opportunities.

The classroom teacher may request a conference with the supervisor. He may wish to seek advice about advanced university work, workshops, conventions, study groups, or other professional growth which he is contemplating. He might feel the need to discuss new or proposed changes in his teaching, or he simply may want to try out some ideas on a sympathetic and knowledgeable person. The beginning teacher often seeks some sort of evaluation of his progress. Other teachers may perceive problems with which they desire help.

The supervisor sometimes initiates the conference. A new supervisor, for example, may schedule individual conferences with the teaching staff in order to meet them individually, to begin to establish sound relationships, to locate common teaching problems, and to identify promising points to initiate supervisory work. Beginning teachers are often asked to come in periodically to discuss their progress, or the supervisor may want to sample teacher opinion regarding a proposed supervisory action before putting it into practice. A teacher may not be aware of serious instructional difficulties and the supervisor may plan a conference with him as a first step toward helping him see the problem for himself.

Preparation for the conference. If the conference is to be a cooperative discussion of some mutually recognized problem, the conference requires preparation by both participants. Both should study available material which deals with the problem. Actually, if one is well-prepared and the other largely uninformed, much of the conference time may be used in instruction until both have some base of knowledge and understanding from which to proceed. In preparation for the conference the teacher will likely have ready access to school records, bring personal observations, obtain samples of student work, and accept responsibility for these and similar data. The supervisor probably will draw upon his resources for securing information regarding experimentation, promising practices and materials, and theoretical bases underlying the problem. If the purpose of the conference is known in advance, such preparation by both participants is essential to the optimum success and satisfaction of the individual conference.

Place of the conference. The unplanned conference, of course, is likely to occur almost anywhere the supervisor and teacher happen to meet and have the opportunity to chat. However, most other individual conferences are held (1) in the teacher's classroom, (2) in the supervisor's office, or (3) in a school conference or social room. The classroom location has some very real advantages. The surroundings are familiar to the teacher; this is his classroom and it gives him a feeling of security and ease. Moreover, instructional materials, class records, and teaching plans are likely to be close at hand. The students, however, should not be present during the discussion, nor should there be constant interruptions from students and staff dropping in.

The supervisor's office may be suitable, for it may be more private than the average classroom. However, cramped supervisory office space in some school systems make private individual conferences impossible. Sometimes telephone interruptions plague the discussion. Ideally the supervisor's office will have reports of research, descriptions of new instructional approaches, samples of promising new materials, and other appropriate resources readily accessible. It will be fitted with comfortable chairs and will have a high degree of privacy. Even so, status differences between teacher and supervisor may be intensified and real cooperative relationships may be inhibited.

Often the social or conference room of the school is the most desirable location. In a sense it is neutral ground; yet it is a part of the school, convenient and accessible to both the supervisor and teacher. The room is likely to be private and free from interruptions, and usually it contains comfortable chairs and is an area usually approved for smoking. Thus it offers a quiet, protected, generally suitable setting for the individual conference.

Time and length of conference. The conference is probably most often scheduled after school. This may not be the most productive time because both supervisor and teacher are likely to be tired after a full day and often are anticipating evening social and family obligations. Sometimes a meeting before school can be arranged. The participants are fresh and more can be accomplished in less time. A preschool conference, however, has rigid time limits set by the opening of school. The planning periods of the teacher commonly are utilized for a meeting and sometimes the supervisor and teacher simply agree to have lunch together. Whenever the conference is arranged, the important thing is to provide privacy and freedom from interruptions.

Ideally the length of the conference is determined, of course, by the nature of the problem and the progress made in its discussion. Most often the discussion must be fitted into the time limits set by the planning period, the lunch period, or by the time until the opening bell. The virtue of an after-school conference is that more time is available. If the discussion seems highly productive, it may be prolonged somewhat without interfering with official duties.

Conducting the conference. The supervisor must develop considerable skill in conducting the conference. His approach may largely determine the degree of productivity of the conference itself and the quality of later teacher-supervisor relationships. Although the nature of individual conferences may vary according to the purpose in mind, successful practices by supervisors indicate several general suggestions.

The basic requirement for a successful individual conference is the establishment of rapport between the teacher and supervisor. One of the significant advantages of this supervisory technique is the opportunity for two professional educational persons to cooperate in dealing with a problem, to share interests, and to really get to know each other. In large systems, especially, new teachers often report the difficulty of becoming closely acquainted with more than a handful of the staff. Everything seems so impersonal; status personnel appear so remote; and satisfying professional relationships are established infrequently. The supervisor who is able to foster rapport will contribute to the teacher's satisfaction on the job, as well as laying the foundation for shared effort in improving instruction.

The conference generally should be informal, sympathetic, and friendly. If the supervisor seeks a peer relationship with the teacher and if he desires a situation in which both participants are able to discuss the possible problems and concerns frankly and without threat, the conference cannot be marked by formality, coldness, and distance. The supervisor, of course, has been a highly successful teacher himself. He possesses certain resources not generally available to all teachers, and he has a degree of perspective and status because of his position. This automatically provides some natural separation. The successful supervisor, however, has learned to set the tone of the conference in a friendly, relaxed way.

It is essential that the teacher's opinions and judgments be respected. Obviously the key to most instructional problems lies in the situation itself, and the teacher is the only trained person who possesses continuing and intimate experience in the particular learning-teaching situation. Moreover, the agent of change is the teacher himself. Improvements will be made only as the teacher makes them in his own classroom. Therefore, the supervisor listens carefully and attentively. The teacher is often too close to his own problem, and one of the most important contributions which the supervisor can make is to help the teacher look at the situation with more perspective and objectivity.

The integrity of the supervisor must be apparent. He accepts and retains the confidences of teachers. Because of his position he is likely to come into possession of confidential information. This he must respect and keep to himself if he would preserve and continue a successful teacher-supervisor relationship. The effective individual conference depends to a substantial degree upon the confidence which teachers develop in the integrity and sincerity of the supervisor.

The conference should be constructive and helpful. When possible, the supervisor points up strengths and areas of improvement, for he knows that positive and constructive supervisory effort generally begins there. The participants wisely focus their attention on future plans for improvement rather than upon past mistakes. Teachers learn far more significantly through their successes than through their failures. The supervisor must be prepared to offer specific help when appropriate. The discussion of the problem may indicate that substitute procedures should be explored. In this case the teacher may look to the supervisor for definite assistance. At this point the full supervisory resources should be made available. For example, promising instructional practices and materials may be brought into the conference for joint consideration of their applicability and probable worth. Specific suggestions may be offered and tentative decisions made. The teacher must feel that the conference has been constructive and helpful, or he may be unwilling to continue.

The purpose of each conference should be clearly understood by both teacher and supervisor. This does not seem too much to ask, because the nature of the discussion, the probable outcome, and the satisfaction of both participants depend upon the expectations which each brings to the meeting. The quality of the interaction and the productivity of the conference hang upon the mutual understanding of the purpose. Such purposes vary greatly. For example, the supervisor may simply wish to meet and become acquainted with a new teacher; a teacher may feel the need to check his impression of a newly emerging problem with an objective, knowledgeable person; or an instructor may wish to report the results of an experimental procedure which had been put into practice through previous teacher-supervisor planning. Whatever the purpose, it provides the basis and justification for the conference.

Follow-up procedures.   An essential part of the supervisor's responsibility in regard to individual conferences is the follow-up activity. Many supervisors take the time to write a report of each scheduled conference. Such a report is mainly for the benefit of the supervisor and takes whatever form he finds most convenient and useful. It may be quite succinct, but it should include such items as (1) date and location of the conference, (2) purpose, (3) main points discussed or problems identified, (4) decisions mutually agreed upon, and (5) commitments regarding future action.

Rather than attempt to rely on memory, such reports form the basis of conference records. These files allow the supervisor to prepare adequately for subsequent conferences, to fulfill commitments which he has made, and to follow through generally with supervisory efforts. The records assist the supervisor in planning his own work, anticipating future demands, and evaluating his service.

Teachers commonly are fully involved with the pressure of teaching and extraclass duties. Therefore, the supervisor must accept the responsibility for preserving momentum and continuity in improvement activities once they are initiated. This means that he needs to see to it that needed materials are delivered, progress checks are made, evaluation and reappraisal are secured, and subsequent planning is accomplished. He follows through on commitments and agreements. He must facilitate the desirable action which should follow the individual conference. Without this bridge to action many conferences would be futile, largely wasted activity.

Well-handled and consistently followed up, the individual conference is potentially one of the most productive of the supervisory procedures. The teachers generally respond well and report a high degree of satisfaction.

Demonstration Teaching

Another supervisory procedure of special value in certain situations is demonstration teaching. Its purpose is generally an attempt to illustrate a recommended method, teaching material, or instructional approach. Supervisors have also used it is a means to provide a sample of the learning-teaching process, which the observing teacher and supervisor may then analyze for supervisory purposes.

For the most part demonstration teaching is more often found at the elementary school level than at the secondary school level. Several probable reasons for this may be suggested. The high school teacher tends to be subject-matter oriented and may look naïvely upon method as simply a means to communicate information from text and teacher to the student. Thus he may seek communication gimmicks rather than looking deeply at ways to provide real learning experiences in the classroom. Elementary teachers, however, are commonly pupil oriented. They are apt to be more willing to focus attention upon the learner and his reactions. For them demonstration teaching and its analysis are more productive and satisfying.

High schools typically are departmentalized. The department head today seldom has the time and opportunity to work effectively as a special supervisor. The central office special supervisor is perceived by the high school teachers as being remote from their teaching situation and probably not aware of their special problems. The general supervisor in their high school obviously is limited in his ability to demonstrate teaching in the various subject areas. This is not true at the elementary school level, for the supervisor is likely to have the training and teaching experience to deal with a wide variety of instructional problems and demands.

Demonstration by whom? As a part of public school supervision, the demonstration teaching may be the work of the supervisor himself, a classroom teacher, a representative of a commercial agency, or a consultant from the office of the county superintendent of schools, the state department of education, or a college or university. Generally, the use of an outside consultant or commercial representative is not wholly satisfactory. An outside expert seldom is intimately acquainted with the concerns of local teachers, conditions and problems in the school, and particular needs which can be met by the use of such demonstration teaching. The representative of a company which produces textbooks, audio-visual equipment, or other instructional materials is naturally interested in their sale. He is specially selected by the company and carefully trained in their use. He is likely to suggest that the success of the lesson is largely due to the materials used, rather than to his own highly developed skill and experience with them.

The supervisor sometimes teaches a lesson—taking over the teacher's class so that the teacher can observe his own students respond to a new procedure or approach. To do this well the supervisor must have established sound relationships with the classroom teacher. He must know and be accepted by the students, and he must understand the planning and teaching which have occurred. Often teachers are able to profit greatly from the experience of seeing another person teaching their class. If the teaching demonstration which they observe is in another classroom with other pupils, they must make certain adaptations and adjustments in thinking about it in relation to their own classes. When the supervisor demonstrates in the teachers' classrooms, they find it easier to compare their teaching, achieve a degree of self-evaluation, and see possible improvements and applications of alternative procedures.

Often the supervisor and teacher arrange to visit another teacher's class. The demonstration teacher carries on his regular instructional duties in his own classroom, and the observers plan with him so that they are able to see the particular learning-teaching activity which has relevance to the supervisory problem that they are discussing. Sometimes they spend half a day; sometimes they stay just long enough to see a complete lesson from start to finish, depending upon the purpose of the observation. A great advantage of this procedure is the fact that both teacher and supervisor are able to plan in advance, see the same sample of teaching, and discuss it subsequently. They may wish, for example, to analyze the reactions of students to an instructional material, check the handling of routine matters, explore the factors which contribute to effective student-teacher interaction, investigate successful techniques of cooperative planning, or observe certain approaches to classroom control. One danger, however, is always present: the skillful teacher whom they observe may work so effectively that the approach used and the specific measures instituted may be hidden in the smoothly functioning classroom activity. Important elements in the situation may go unnoticed because of the excellence of the teaching. Also, an inexperienced teacher may become discouraged and despair of ever achieving the exemplary performance observed.

Procedure. Demonstration teaching must be oriented to the needs and concerns of the teacher involved. The supervisor and teacher identify specific problems and plan to use the technique of demonstration teaching to help resolve these difficulties.

In most cases demonstration teaching is used with individual faculty members rather than with groups, because it would be difficult to find a number of teachers who have exactly the same instructional problems and who could profit equally well from observing a particular demonstration lesson. It has also been noted that the larger the group of observers, the more artificial the classroom situation becomes. Moreover, the demonstrating teacher is likely, in spite of himself, to give a performance for his colleagues rather than illustrate a fairly normal learning-teaching situation.

All demonstration teaching, as a supervisory procedure, requires careful planning and preparation. The supervisor and teacher confer in advance of the observation, for the purpose of the demonstration must be clearly understood. It is obvious that the observer will profit more if he has certain things in mind for which to look. He should know the objectives of the lesson, the content to be presented, the nature of the activities to be used, and the evaluative measures to be employed.

The supervisor and teacher should establish the nature of the demonstration. The lesson may be suggestive, try-out, or experimental. It may be a recommended procedure or model given for the benefit of an inexperienced teacher, or it might simply show an experienced teacher meeting the normal instructional demands in a fairly typical classroom.

Each demonstration should be followed by a discussion session as soon as possible. In this meeting the supervisor and teacher compare impressions, discuss the application of principles, evaluate the apparent success of procedures or materials used, explore applications or adaptations potentially useful to the observing teacher, and clarify misunderstandings. Sometimes the demonstrating teacher may be involved at least to the extent of explaining his attempts, his aims, and his judgment of the success of the lesson. This post-demonstration conference offers the supervisor an opportunity to deepen teacher understanding, to reinforce desires to improve, and to move the teacher to action.

Demonstration teaching is normally most often used with beginning teachers, although it may be extremely helpful with some experienced instructors. It is a specialized supervisory procedure requiring much time and detailed planning; yet its potential benefits are obvious and unquestionably worthwhile.

Planned Interschool and Intraschool Visitation

Teacher visitation is similar to demonstration teaching, for it provides the opportunity for teachers to visit other teachers within their own school or in neighboring schools. Although usually not extensively and regularly used, it is an old and respected supervisory device. It is usually less formal and less carefully planned than demonstration teaching. Large numbers of teachers, however, may be involved. Supervisors may play a less vital role; yet the procedure provides the important possibility of teachers' working together, learning from each other, and sharing their professional experience.

Kinds of visitation. Both interschool and intraschool visitation may be utilized. Visitation within the school itself (intraschool) is more feasible in large schools than it is in small ones. The small high school, for instance, is handicapped because there may not be a single teacher in some of the academic departments who is both willing to have people visit him and who is teaching so excellently or trying something so new and significant that he is a proper subject for teacher visitation. Small elementary schools are subject to the same sort of limitations. All schools, however, may find visitation among other schools (interschool) possible and rewarding.

Intraschool visitation is especially useful with inexperienced teachers. The supervisor arranges for the beginning instructor to observe a skillful teacher or sometimes several expert teachers in action. The neophyte faculty member is eager to learn, poses no threat to an older staff member, and can profitably observe the teaching of a wide range of teachers in the school. This practice usually has fewer deleterious effects on teacher morale than when experienced teachers are urged to visit other teachers within the school.

Some supervisors, however, find it desirable to encourage intraschool visitation upon request; that is, the teacher who feels the need will be able to plan to visit for a particular purpose. The supervisor plans with the teacher in advance, arranges an appropriate visit, and then confers with the teacher regarding the experience. This practice is patently more likely to be productive than the occasional practice of requiring all teachers to make visitations, whether or not they have a conscious purpose for doing so. In schools where experimentation is in progress, teachers often visit each other's classrooms in order to secure ideas, refine procedures, and evaluate the changes. At the secondary school level such intraschool visitation is commonly arranged during the teacher's planning period or study hall period. In the elementary school the supervisor or a substitute may take the teacher's class so that he is free to make the observation.

Interschool visitation requires more extensive planning by supervisor and administrator, but it opens up great possibilities for productive experiences. Some schools may for one day not hold classes, so that all teachers may take advantage of the opportunity to visit other schools. Careful planning and organization is essential so that every teacher is able to observe something of value. The task of establishing purposes of the visit with each individual teacher and the finding and arranging of suitable classrooms in other schools is a formidable one.

Visitation on a smaller scale is more often done. Selected teachers are encouraged to visit exceptionally fine teachers in neighboring schools. A committee which is exploring the possibilities of a new instructional approach may observe the teaching in a school which is already using the new procedure. Interschool visitation, of course, requires the use of substitutes or supply teachers in order to release the visiting teachers.

Although visitation most often is made in classes and situations closely similar to the teacher's own classroom assignment, other kinds may be valuable. For example, the fourth grade teacher may visit classes above and below his level in order to understand better the total elementary school curriculum. The high school teacher may follow some of his pupils as they move from class to class through the school day in order to gain insight into the nature of the total school experience of students. Teachers may visit extra-class activities as organized and carried on in other schools. A variety of such procedures may be useful to the supervisor, depending upon the needs of the teacher and the purpose of the visitation.

Arrangements. In visitation the problem of arranging a productive experience is vital. The supervisor must plan closely with the principal of the school or schools involved, must prepare teachers in advance of the observation, and must follow up the experience in order to insure the most value from the activity.

Teachers need to prepare for the visit. They must have a worthwhile purpose in mind and they should have specific and significant things to observe. The teacher to be visited must be informed of the impending visit. He should also know the needs of the visitor. In this way the supervisor insures against his teacher having nothing to observe but a full day of review activity, workbook assignments, motion pictures, or unit examinations.

The host teacher must have consented to the visit and be willing to discuss his instruction with the visiting teacher afterwards. This post-visitation conference is essential, for it provides the opportunity for the demonstrating teacher to explain his aims and procedures to the observer. It allows the visitor to ask questions, clarify impressions, and secure specific assistance. A follow-up discussion is commonly held in a committee, departmental, or faculty meeting in which the visiting teacher brings the results of his experience back to his own colleagues. In the case of intraschool visitation a supervisor-teacher conference provides needed follow-up.

Other Individual Supervisory Procedures

The supervisory person must learn to work in many different ways to accomplish various purposes. Of the many possibilities, several other supervisory approaches are worthy of brief mention.

Lesson plans.   All teachers must meet and solve the problem of planning and arranging the elements of meaningful and effective lessons. This is a crucial facet of the successful teacher's art. Great differences among student groups, schools, and teachers make the common practice of textbook teaching undesirable and ineffective. Although some group approaches may be helpful, the supervisor can be especially effective working with individual teachers in relation to their instructional planning. Shared supervisor-teacher planning requires special supervisor competencies.

In order to effect emancipation from textbook domination, the supervisor must be able to help the individual gain experience and skill in constructing resource units, teaching units, and lesson plans which have unity, are adapted to the particular students involved, and include a variety of useful teaching materials. Beginning teachers especially need to develop security in planning work independent of the adopted text. Most teachers, at one time or another, welcome help in organizing activities and materials around a central idea, theme, problem, or issue which has significant appeal to their students. They may recognize the advantages of the unit concept but may find it difficult to separate their thinking from the systematic textbook presentation (based on the logic of the subject) or to rise above day-to-day planning and piecemeal teaching (based on expediency).

Sound planning, whether it be a long resource unit or a daily lesson plan, centers on a stated list of carefully considered objectives. These objectives provide the justification for the learning-teaching activities and indicate the kinds of evaluative procedures necessary for assessing progress. Psychological principles of unity, motivation, progression, momentum, and closure should guide the planning. Assistance is needed in helping teachers search for chunks of subject matter, vital generalizations, discrete skills, or pivotal ideas to use as organizing centers. Often supervisors have set up planning laboratories which include such helpful items as resource and teaching units, logs or series of daily lesson plans used in actual teaching, curriculum guides, course outlines, bibliographies of supplementary books and materials, and lists of recommended community resources. Teachers may be encouraged to try out several resource units from the collection and then to use the other items in planning units of their own.

Professional library. Supervisors commonly seek to provide an array of publications for the use of individual teachers. Depending on the size and resources of the school, this may range from a single teacher's shelf in the school library or principal's office to a sizable collection housed in the teachers' planning room or materials center. Such a professional library may include current books on topics of general import to the whole field of education, the particular level of education which the school serves, and special subject-matter areas. The collection may also contain selected nonprofessional works. It is likely to include journals and yearbooks published by professional associations and which cover a variety of special and general interests.

Teachers can reasonably be expected to belong to certain professional organizations closely related to their teaching responsibilities, and they would already have copies of some periodicals. The professional library should, therefore, subscribe to publications less readily accessible. Reports of curriculum experimentation, source books of new and promising practices, summaries of research findings, and pamphlets describing trends and developments in teaching may also be included. Ideally, the supervisor will involve teachers in the selection and purchase of new titles.

Planned travel and study. Individual teachers regularly seek out the supervisor for counsel and recommendations regarding planned travel and study. It is clear that travel has both educative and therapeutic values for the teacher. The high school English teacher who has the opportunity to visit Britain is bound to improve his teaching of English literature. The social studies teacher, after a trip to Washington, D.C., is apt to breathe more life and vitality into some of his instruction. In addition, the planned vacation can release tensions and renew enthusiasm for teaching. New and different surroundings and activities prove to be enormously beneficial after a long and demanding school year.

Advanced or continuing education is commonly used by teachers to fill in gaps in their preparation for teaching, to keep up with current developments in their subject field, to explore new instructional procedures and trends, to expand their personal horizons, to satisfy nonprofessional interests, and to prepare for advanced educational positions. The supervisor can often provide valuable guidance in regard to appropriate summer school and extension course work. An increasing number of universities are offering workshops and carefully planned courses especially for teachers. These offerings provide specific help with the problems and concerns of classroom teachers. Sometimes a large school district will arrange with a university to offer a particular course for the benefit of that district. Often the course is financed completely by the district and is concerned with the special problems of its schools.

Many teachers also need assistance in choosing advanced degrees suitable to their vocational aspirations and in selecting appropriate collegiate institutions. The supervisor can perform a necessary and vital role in such planning.

CHAPTER VIII

Appraisal of the Supervisor's Work

Evaluation of the work of the supervisor is an especially difficult process, for the cause and effect relationship is seldom clear. Apparent improvement in learning and teaching may result from a variety of forces, only one of which is the supervisory program of the school. Moreover, properly instituted supervision may be a relatively subtle activity. A significant aspect of the supervisor's art is the ability to set in motion certain processes, remove blocks to progress, provide encouragement and support, stimulate thinking, and offer casual suggestions which result in teachers' instituting changes which they accept as their own. These improvements, of course, are their own if they have analyzed their problems, explored possible alternatives, and decided upon a course of action, even though they may have utilized supervisory resources and assistance. The effective supervisor is a person who is more interested in significant and lasting teacher growth and productivity of learning than in personal publicity or aggrandizement.

Appraisal of the supervisor's work must take many forms and use a variety of approaches. It is essential that this task be undertaken so that the supervisor may revise and improve his methods and continually enhance his effectiveness. He must secure evidence of the results of his work.

Measures of Pupil Learning

The success or failure of supervision is inevitably tied to its overall aim. Thus an evaluation of the results of the learning-teaching process would seem to provide useful data. If the evidence indicated that learning had increased significantly over that of past years, one might feel justified in concluding that the recent supervisory procedures, in the absence of other obvious variables such as a dramatic shift in the quality of instructional staff, deserve some of the credit. The evaluation, however, would be imprecise, because no direct and obvious relationship could be established. In-school learning, of course, is affected by the teacher, the home, peer groups, and other educative agencies in the community. The learning-teaching process is infinitely complex and subject to many influences. If, however, a supervisor has noted poor pupil achievement in a learning area and if he has instituted appropriate supervision measures and found subsequent achievement in this area to be greatly improved, he could probably conclude justifiably that his contribution had been worthwhile.

Some persons have used student scores on standardized tests in an effort to determine the value of supervision. For example, Franseth [1] reported a study made in Georgia which compared pupil achievement in fifth, sixth, and seventh grades between very similar schools, some of which were supervised and some unsupervised. The results indicated that the students achieved more in schools which had the benefit of supervision than in those which did not. This approach would seem to have potential value if adapted for use within an individual school.

Instead of relying on hunch or intuition, the supervisor might well use a variety of evaluative procedures to assess the learning of students in relation to desired educational objectives. Upon finding weaknesses, he would work cooperatively with teachers to find direct and forceful ways to improve the situation. Subsequent evaluation of pupil progress toward these particular aims would indicate the success of the teachers' efforts and, indirectly, the effect of the supervisor's work. Such a program of appraisal should, of course, go beyond standardized tests to include such procedures as teacher observation of pupil behavior, rating scales, anecdotal records, and student self-evaluation.

Teacher Use of Instructional Methods and Materials

Another approach to the evaluation of the supervisor's work seeks evidence regarding the more effective use of teaching methods and materials. Most supervisors, as they work with teachers to im-

---

[1] Jane Franseth, *Learning to Supervise Schools: An Appraisal of the Georgia Program* (Washington, D.C.: U.S. Office of Education, Government Printing Office, 1952).

prove learning and teaching, note changes in instruction—that is, teachers use new materials, refine procedures, and adopt new approaches. Unless records are kept, however, no systematic appraisal is possible; and the supervisor must rely on hunch, general impression, or memory.

Teacher visitation will reveal evidence of improved instruction. The supervisor, as he observes in the classroom, notes the use of new teaching materials and recommended procedures. He recognizes teacher growth, especially in regard to previous problems and difficulties with which teacher and supervisor are cooperatively seeking to deal. He looks for changed attitudes, increased self confidence, and security in the teacher's approach to his classroom duties. The results of such observations, when related to supervisory measures, form one basis for evaluation.

Conferences with individual teachers allow the supervisor to gain insight into the teacher's developing knowledge of a wide range of possible instructional materials, improved understanding of their use, feelings regarding changed instructional methods, and willingness to work for improvement. A series of such discussions, spread over a year or more, reveals teacher development and improvement as related to supervisory activity. For example, an inexperienced teacher may begin teaching by following the textbook slavishly. The supervisor, in conferring with him, discovers that this is largely due to a lack of self-confidence in his own ability to plan the classwork. Subsequent teacher-supervisor planning and discussion results in the decision of the new instructor to try some lessons which they have organized. As a result the supervisor notes a significant change in the teacher's use of materials adapted to his particular classes. He also notes the teacher's increasing confidence and skill in independent planning. The reports of the individual conferences placed in a supervisory file provide an indication of the worth of supervision efforts.

Teacher self-evaluation of use of methods and materials may also be used. Supervisors provide occasions for individuals or groups of teachers to discuss their instructional procedures. Departmental meetings or grade level groups may be encouraged to devote a series of meetings to a self-examination of the teaching of various aspects of their work. More formal self-evaluation, using questionnaires or checklists, may assist teachers in making judgments of their own work in the classroom. Supervisors may use the results in assessing their contributions.

Most teachers, however, tend to use a single criterion of the success or failure of the new classroom procedure. Unless more structured evaluative instruments assist them in applying a variety of standards, they tend to make judgments based on perceived student interest and enthusiasm. Brickell, in his study of educational change in the state of New York, found that:

> Instructional innovations are almost always evaluated by observing the reactions of the students while they are receiving the new instruction. In the eyes of the practitioner, no other evidence outweighs student reaction as a measure of success.[2]

An adaptation of parts of the Evaluative Criteria,[3] or of its elementary school equivalent, may be used to evaluate the instruction of the school in relation to its stated educational objectives and to accepted principles and practices of teaching. This will provide evidence regarding teacher use of methods and materials as measured against a recognized set of standards. Other surveys of the use of certain materials and procedures or aspects of the academic and extraclass program will secure useful data. Improvement noted from one survey to the next over a period of time may reveal possible benefits of the supervisor's labors.

With all these approaches the supervisor must keep adequate records. His records allow him to take an organized look at the state of teaching in his school as related to his work in the direction of improving teacher use of methods and materials.

Teacher Morale

One aspect of the school of great importance to administrative and supervisory personnel is the quality of teacher morale. Thus the supervisor seeks to institute procedures which will sustain and further improve the morale. It is especially difficult to appraise the results of such procedures, for the school board, administration,

---

[2] Henry M. Brickell, *Organizing New York State for Educational Change* (Albany, N.Y.: Commissioner of Education, State Education Department, 1961), p. 33.

[3] *Evaluative Criteria,* (Washington, D.C.: National Study of Secondary-School Evaluation, 1960).

pressure groups in the community, publicity given to attacks and criticisms of the schools, and small special interest groups within the faculty may suddenly and dramatically affect the situation. Nevertheless, the supervisor constantly seeks to assess the changing quality of morale among the teachers with whom he works.

Improved morale is evident in such symptoms as expressed teacher satisfaction with teaching assignment and colleagues, increased social interaction among teachers, greater commitment to all school objectives, and a growing feeling of shared responsibility for the improvement of the total program of the school. Behavior of teachers in committees and groups may reveal positive growth toward a willingness and ability to work cooperatively with more productive results. Human relations skills, relatively mature group process relationships, and mutually supportive actions are observed. Teachers increasingly may feel free to raise questions, admit weaknesses, try out new ideas, and seek assistance. Supervisors recognize the vital importance of high staff morale, work toward improving it, and attempt to evaluate their efforts in this regard.

Specific Supervisory Procedures

An obvious approach to the appraisal of the worth of supervisory activity is the evaluation of specific procedures. The results, however, must be handled with some caution. It is sometimes hard to retain perspective of the overall program if individual procedures are evaluated separately. Of course, each is a part of the total. On the one hand, the effect of a single procedure may not be evident, but the total combined services may make a significant difference in improving instruction. On the other hand, one supervisory technique may show substantial results in one area, but the total program may be poorly balanced with little or no attention given to certain other problem areas. Nevertheless, most supervisors feel it is important to seek appraisal of the specific procedures which they use.

Evaluation of group work may be secured by asking participants to assess the quality and perceived worth of the experiences which they have had in the group. Checklists and questionnaires are often especially useful in this regard. These secure teacher comments and reactions in relation to various aspects of the group process and their role in it. Sometimes a group evaluator is chosen. It is his task to observe the group activity, keep participation records and charts, note the quality and quantity of the contributions of consultants or resource persons, judge the nature of the working atmosphere in the group, and assess the leadership displayed. Analysis of the minutes or reports kept of committee meetings or work groups provides a basis for appraisal. Evaluation discussions may be set up in which the group members discuss the group procedure, aspects which they liked and disliked, and their degree of satisfaction.

The productivity of group procedures may also be indicated by the documents resulting from the procedures. Lists of recommendations, plans for action, resource units, course outlines, suggested curricular changes, research reports, handbooks, policy statements, and progress reports are some of the materials which groups may produce. These may be examined and, when related to the purposes and goals of the groups, form a basis for evaluating the various procedures.

Classroom visitation by the supervisor, individual conferences with teachers, demonstration teaching, teacher visitation, and other supervisory procedures may be evaluated cooperatively by supervisor and teacher as an integral part of the supervision activity itself. For example, the conference following teacher visitation in a neighboring school should, as a part of the process, provide for a discussion of the visit and the teacher's reactions to it. Enumeration of subsequent plans to try out ideas in the classroom, look into new instructional materials, send for descriptions of new programs, study research findings, form study groups, and suggest new items for action in faculty committees will indicate both potential and achieved results. Teacher growth is evident in increased awareness, augumented understanding, new interests and enthusiasm, and willingness to improve. Sometimes the supervisor may obtain the assistance of the administrator in evaluating his individual procedures. The principal may discuss the supervision with teachers singly or in groups. Often supervisory appraisal can become a topic for discussion at such faculty gatherings as department or grade level committees and staff meetings. The results are subsequently reported to the supervisor.

Evaluation of the total supervisory program in relation to its parts may be secured by a comprehensive survey of staff opinion.

Teachers and other educational personnel are asked to rate various supervisory procedures as to how helpful they were and as to how they have effected improvements in the program of the school. These surveys may ask for identification of those activities which appear most helpful and least helpful, or they may require a rating of the degree of satisfaction which teachers feel regarding the total services as well as each of its parts. A variety of discussions in meetings of the whole faculty, committees, and work groups may supplement and augment the survey in order to secure more comprehensive evaluation.

Role of Teachers and Supervisor in Improving Instruction

One important sign of a mature, well-established supervisory program is a faculty, supervisor, and administrator who work together smoothly and effectively to improve instruction. It is especially important for the teachers and the supervisory personnel to work out mutually satisfying relationships. Thus any appraisal of the work of the supervisor must seek evidence of improved perception on the part of faculty members.

Such evaluation will attempt to secure insight into teacher expectations in regard to supervision. It is revealing to discover what the teachers feel to be the proper role of supervision and to compare this to the conscious aims of the supervisor himself. Ideally, the faculty members and the supervisor should accept the premise that all are seeking the same ultimate goal of more productive learning and teaching. Moreover, they should recognize the necessity of cooperating to this end. The supervisor should be viewed as a staff person with little or no administrative status and authority. The teachers need to see the office of the supervisor and the services which he offers as resources and assistance made available to them to help them fulfill their classroom responsibilities more effectively. Thus evaluation might begin simply with an appraisal of the faculty members' knowledge of what resources are available. Beyond this, deeper insight into teacher attitudes and perceptions is provided by such criteria as evidence of their willingness to use these resources, degree of enthusiasm regarding teacher-supervisor conferences, minimal fear and apprehension toward visitation, response to suggestions, sustained interest and enthusiasm in cooperative planning, frankness and openness in discussions with the supervisor, and inclination to participate in attacking group problems.

Supervisor's Self-Evaluation

The successful supervisor carries out continuous self-evaluation of his work. In this way he is in a position to assess his growth on the job. He checks his activities periodically to be sure that they display a balanced approach to the needs of the school. He evaluates apparent progress and results in relation to his objectives of supervision.

One of the most helpful procedures in self-evaluation is the simple habit of keeping a log or diary of how time is spent. The supervisor succinctly notes his work during each day. Typically this is done in simple outline form, although some supervisors may include such items as amount of time spent, comments and reactions by teachers, apparent results, and reminders about follow-up procedures. The main thing to remember is that this record is for the supervisor's own benefit. Thus it will take whatever form seems to be most convenient and useful to him. When this supervisory effort is conscientiously carried out during the entire year, the journal provides the basis for a sound analysis of the supervisor's work. It tells the story of what he did with his time and energy. As such it helps him review his labors more objectively and systematically. When he sits down to scan the log at the end of the school year or periodically during the year, he is able to pick out recurring patterns, aspects of sequence, overuse and underuse of certain procedures, possibilities which may have been overlooked, opportunities realized or missed, and the like. In the day-to-day press of his duties such analyses are difficult, if not impossible. He may need to justify to the administration and, especially, to himself the time spent in relation to the apparent outcomes.

The supervisor's files contain records of his individual conferences and classroom visitation of teachers. When these are filed in sequence for each teacher, they become a series of small, fairly detailed case studies of his work with individual faculty members. These files offer a means for analysis of supervisory efforts. They are, of course, regularly consulted in preparing for subsequent conferences and in following through on commitments. Individual progress, however, often seems slow and minimal. Nevertheless, evidence of small progress in each of many such cases adds up to substantial overall results. Similarly, a study of group records, progress reports, and resulting documents allows judgments to be made of the supervisor's own contributions in groups which he had a part in instituting. The process of supervision is typically covert; its results are often not obvious and clear. Thus such records are essential in reporting the achievements of supervision in the schools.

Self-evaluation may also be accomplished by the supervisor's rating himself against a criterion listing of desirable supervisory behavior or a checklist consisting of a series of significant questions. For example, a report of the Southern States Work Conference [4] suggests a checklist which requires a supervisor to judge the degree to which he had displayed certain behaviors. For example, he must check "often," "seldom," or "never" in regard to such questions as "Am I giving praise often and emphasizing the good aspects of a teacher's work?" and "Am I providing opportunities for teachers to develop potential leadership?" Crosby [5] proposes that the supervisor seek evidence which will provide answers to the following questions:

> Has rapport between participants deepened?
> Have teachers developed a greater freedom in expressing opinions and sharing ideas?
> Does leadership move more freely and frequently from person to person?
> Is there greater teacher initiative?
> Are teachers better able to identify their own problems?
> Do they seek help more frequently?
> Are teachers better able to identify the needs of boys and girls and meet them in more satisfying ways?
> Have the supervisor, principal, and others in appointed leadership roles grown through the common experience in working more effectively with people, in increasing professional "know how," in broadening and deepening insight and understanding the problems in education, in teacher-education, and in human relationships?

---

[4] *Educational Supervision—A Leadership Service* (Tallahassee, Fla.: Southern States Work Conference, Florida State Department of Education, 1955), pp. 73–74.

[5] Muriel Crosby, *Supervision as Co-operative Action* (New York: Appleton-Century-Crofts, Inc., 1957), p. 117.

Many similar lists of criteria [6] and pivotal questions [7] have been proposed for the self-evaluation of supervisors. Some of them are highly detailed and call attention to many specific aspects of the work of supervision. They may be valuable when used as a total checklist, or they may be abbreviated or otherwise adapted to suit the purposes of the supervisor. Their main purpose, of course, is to assist the supervisor to look systematically and searchingly at himself and his own procedures.

In the process of appraising the overall work of the supervisor, a number of different approaches are valuable in securing a variety of pertinent evidence. Final judgments of quality, worth, improvement, or progress, however, must be made in relation to (1) the aims and directions of supervision and (2) the specific educational context within which it operates.

An essential aspect of supervision, therefore, is to establish the purposes of the supervisor. These, in some cases, may be the personal aims of the supervisor; yet, ideally, the administrator, the faculty, and the supervisor share in the task of formulating and clarifying purposes of the program for improving instruction. This preparation may take the form of a list of specific areas which are singled out for special attention. It might be an enumeration of weak points in the curriculum which need much work. The statement may indicate problems which the staff cooperatively has decided to focus on during the school year. Or it may be a comprehensive list of long-range purposes of supervision. Many schools profit from the formulation of overall purposes and a yearly statement of specific points of attack or areas of emphasis. In any event, the aims provide essential standards for evaluation of the results of supervision. Appraisal is most meaningful when productivity is established by checking how well the supervisor and staff actually accomplished what they set out to do.

The evaluation of supervision according to an ideal set of cri-

---

[6] See, for example, Hanne J. Hicks, *Educational Supervision in Principle and Practice* (New York: The Ronald Press Company, 1960), pp. 418–21; and *Leadership for Improving Instruction*, 1960 Yearbook (Washington, D.C.: Association for Supervision and Curriculum Development, National Education Association, 1960), pp. 164–68.

[7] See, for example, R. C. Hammock and R. S. Owings, *Supervising Instruction in Secondary Schools* (New York: McGraw-Hill Book Company, Inc., 1955), pp. 224–25; and Kimball Wiles, *Supervision for Better Schools* (Englewood Cliffs, N.J.: Prentice-Hall, Inc., 1950), pp. 270–78.

teria is valuable in checking the perspective, vision, and maturity of the supervisor. It may not, however, do justice to a supervisory person without also considering his personality, training, and experience, as well as the nature of the educational situation itself. For example, the supervisor being evaluated may be inexperienced or new to his job in a school system where supervision in any substantial sense has never existed before. Certainly his ways of working, the response by the educational staff, and observable results are likely to vary greatly from those of an experienced supervisor working efficiently with school personnel who are convinced of the worth of supervision and used to his procedures. It is necessary to know the situation. Such items as financial resources, degree of administrative support, quality and stability of the teaching staff, level of faculty morale, and past history of supervision in the district are essential to judicious appraisal of the supervisor's work.

Educational supervision is important to the continuing upgrading of learning and teaching in the public schools. Although it is an old and valued service, new visions of a more productive role, improved ways of working, more constructive teacher-supervisor relationships, and approaches to evaluation indicate further developments which will enhance the stature and increase the potential contributions of the supervisor.

Bibliography

Adams, H. P. and F. G. Dickey, *Basic Principles of Supervision*. New York: American Book Company, 1955.

Association for Supervision and Curriculum Development, Yearbooks and Bulletins. Write the Association for list. 1201 16th Street, N.W., Washington, D.C.

Barr, A. S., "Teacher Effectiveness and Its Correlates," *Journal of Experimental Education*, No. 30 (September, 1961), 134–56.

Bartky, J. A., *Supervision as Human Relations*. Boston: D. C. Heath & Company, 1953.

Burnham, R. M. and M. L. King, *Supervision in Action*. Washington, D.C.: Association for Supervision and Curriculum Development, National Education Association, 1961.

Burton, W. H., and L. J. Brueckner, *Supervision: A Social Process,* 3rd ed. New York: Appleton-Century-Crofts, Inc., 1955.

"Continuing Growth for the Teacher," *Educational Leadership,* No. 20 (November, 1962), 85–135.

Corey, S. M., *Action Research to Improve School Practices*. New York: Bureau of Publications, Teachers College, Columbia University, 1953.

Crosby, Muriel, *Supervision as Co-operative Action*. New York: Appleton-Century-Crofts, Inc., 1957.

Douglass, H. R., R. K. Bent, and C. W. Boardman, *Democratic Supervision in Secondary Schools,* 2nd ed. Boston: Houghton Mifflin Company, 1961.

Educational Supervision—A Leadership Service. Tallahassee, Fla.: Southern States Work Conference, Florida State Department of Education, 1955.

Elsbree, W. S. and H. J. McNally, *Elementary School Administration and Supervision,* 2nd ed. New York: American Book Company, 1959.

Gage, N. L., ed. *Handbook of Research on Teaching,* A Project of the American Educational Research Association. Chicago: Rand McNally & Co., 1963.

Group Planning in Education, 1945 Yearbook. Washington, D.C.: Department of Supervision and Curriculum Development, National Education Association, 1945.

Group Processes in Supervision. Washington, D.C.: Association for Supervision and Curriculum Development, National Education Association, 1948.

Gwynn, J. Minor, *Theory and Practice of Supervision*. New York: Dodd, Mead & Co., 1961.

Hammock, R. C. and R. S. Owings, *Supervising Instruction in Secondary Schools*. New York: McGraw-Hill Book Company, Inc., 1955.

Hicks, H. J., *Educational Supervision in Principle and Practice*. New York: The Ronald Press Company, 1960.

Hullfish, H. G. and P. G. Smith, *Reflective Thinking: The Method of Education*. New York: Dodd, Mead & Co., 1961.

In-service Education for Teachers, Supervisors, and Administrators, Fifty-Sixth Yearbook. Chicago: The National Society for the Study of Education, 1957.

Leadership for Improving Instruction, 1960 Yearbook. Washington, D.C.: Association for Supervision and Curriculum Development, National Education Association, 1960.

Lucio, W. H. and J. D. McNeil, *Supervision: A Synthesis of Thought and Action*. New York: McGraw-Hill Book Company, Inc., 1962.

Manlove, D. C., "The Principal's Role in Improving Instruction," *NASSP Bulletin*, No. 44 (December, 1962), 1–5.

Swearingen, Mildred E., *Supervision of Instruction: Foundations and Dimensions*. Boston: Allyn and Bacon, Inc., 1962.

Wiles, Kimball, *Supervision for Better Schools*. Englewood Cliffs, N.J.: Prentice-Hall, Inc., 1950.

Yauch, W. A., *Helping Teachers Understand Principals*. New York: Appleton-Century-Crofts, Inc., 1957.

Zimiles, Herbert, "Mental Health and School Personnel," *Review of Educational Research*, No. 32 (December, 1962), 484–94.

Index